D1043478
C or P

coke

OR

pepsi?

coke OR pepsi? FOREVER!

What do you really know about your friends?

FINE print PUBLISHING

coke OR pepsi? FOREVER!

Written and designed by
Mickey & Cheryl Gill

Fine Print Publishing Company
P.O. Box 916401
Longwood, Florida 32791-6401

ISBN 978-189295161-8

This book is printed on acid-free paper.
Created in the U.S.A. & Printed in China

4 6 8 10 9 7 5 3

coke-or-pepsi.com

Pass this book around to all your friends. Each friend has a chance to answer some pretty cool questions.

See what you have in common.

Find out what makes you different.

Some answers might shock you.

PLEASE PASS THIS BOOK BACK TO
Name
makes me laugh hard.
Favorite thing that comes in a bag?
Castle in the mountains
Cottage in the woods
Birthday
City you were born in?
Moonlight
Sunshine
Coolest animal with whiskers?

Something hanging in your closet that you never wear?

Fave thing that comes on a stick?

○ Shrink to the size of an ant
○ Supersize to the size of an elephant?

Question you love to ask? ______________________________

____

○ **Diamonds** ○ **Pearls?**

1. Name ( )

2. ○ Cinnamon ○ Fruity ○ Minty gum?

3. What do you love about yourself? ____________________

4. Where were you last time you used mustard? ____________________

5. The last paper I wrote for a class was about ____________________

____________________.

6. I could never eat ____________________ again and be OK.

7. TV show you most belong on? ____________________

8. WOULD YOU RATHER BE THE ○ STAR ON A LOSING TEAM ○ WORST ON A STAR TEAM?

9. Ever carved anything in a tree? ○ Yes ○ No

10. ○ Swim with the dolphins ○ Pet a manatee?

11. Would you rather be a ○ giant ○ pixie?

12. ○ Fuzzy socks ○ Warm slippers?

13. Hot chocolate ○ with ○ without marshmallows?

14. Good at sneaking up on people? ○ Not really ○ Kind of ○ Absolutely!

15. Scariest thing you've done on purpose? ____________________

16. New pair of ○ jeans ○ shoes?

17. If I could ____________________, I would be thrilled.

18. Age you turned on fave birthday? ( )

19. Something you would love to see? ____________________

20. Which is worse? ○ Really sad ○ Out-of-control mad

Potato chips
French fries?
coke
OR
pepsi?
Fashionable
Casual?
Sunset
Sunrise?
classic
Brownies
Chocolate chip cookies?
Best holiday?
Fave actor?
Fave actress?
One word to describe you?
Big Mac
Whopper?
Gold
Silver?
coke-or-pepsi.com

forever

1. Name ~~megan~~arin

2. ◯ Skinny jeans ◯ Jeggings ◯ Neither? (checked: Skinny jeans)

3. *Happiest color?* neon orange

4. What were you doing in the last photo taken of you? kissy face

5. Where were you? on my couch

6. Know how to cook? ◯ **No** ◯ **A little** ◯ **Yes** (checked: A little)

7. If yes to #6, what's your specialty? cakes

8. Are you usually ◯ cold ◯ hot? (checked: hot)

9. Famous person you admire most? megan

10. DO HORROR MOVIES FRIGHTEN YOU? ◯ **NOT REALLY** ◯ **YES, NIGHTMARES!** (checked: Yes, nightmares!)

11. Fave outfit to relax in? leggings, sweatshirt

12. Ever shoot a spitball? ◯ Yes ◯ Gross, no!

13. Favorite thing that comes in your mail? packages.

14. Sprinkles ◯ always make me happy ◯ are kinda overrated. (checked: always make me happy)

15. Any phobias or fears? ◯ Nope ◯ Yes, I'm afraid of dark & alone. (checked: Yes)

16. ◯ Drama queen ◯ Cool, calm, and collected?

17. What do you crave? swish

18. Drink after other people? ◯ Yeah ◯ Sometimes ◯ Never! Germs! (checked: Sometimes)

19. Ever encountered a bat? ◯ Yes ◯ No (checked: Yes)

20. What do you hear right now? TV

FEAR

Ahh! You're going to wear that?

Scare-crow! Caww!

1. Name noemi

2. Afraid to cross bridges? ☑ Yes ○ No

3. Can you wiggle your ears without using your hands? ☑ No ○ Yes

4. Do you ○ give in ☑ get your way?

5. LAST THING YOU SOLD FOR YOUR SCHOOL? cookies

6. Go to the library? ☑ No ○ Yes

7. Longest word you know? supercalifragilisticexpialidocious

8. **Can you hang a spoon from your nose?** ○ **Yes** ☑ **No** ○ **Huh?**

9. Best food with a glass of milk? Cookies

10. Gold ○ fish ☑ bracelet?

11. **Any strange talent?** ☑ **No** ○ **Yes, I** ________.

12. Spend the night in a haunted house? ☑ NO! ○ Sure, I don't believe.

13. It's scary how much I like ~~[illegible]~~ ASpforeaten.

14. Give good manicures? ☑ Yes ○ No

15. Favorite reality show? survivor voice americas got talent

16. Scrambled eggs are ☑ yummy ○ frightening.

17. Worst thing about your brother(s)/sister(s)? mean

18. Best thing about your brother(s)/sister(s)? Love

19. **LOVE A GOOD MYSTERY?** ○ **YES!** ☑ **NAH**

20. Think you're creative? ☑ Yes ○ A little ○ Not really

Name

1. swim with a huge, harmless whale in the ocean, would you? ○Yes ○No, but I would swim with ______________________.

2. slow down time, which event would you slow down? ______________________

3. add sisters or brothers to your family, which genders and ages would you choose?

____

4. have absolutely anything for dinner tonight, what would you pick? ______________________

____

5. do one fun thing with an alien visiting our planet, what would it be? ______________________

____

6. become any object for just one day, what would you be? Why? ______________________

____

7. be an exchange student for one year anywhere in the world, which country would you visit? ______________________

8. be great friends with someone from the past, who would you choose? Why?

____

9. do absolutely anything for just one year, what would you do? ______________________

____

10. change your last name, without hurting your parents' feelings, would you?

○ No ○ Yes, I would change it to ______________________.

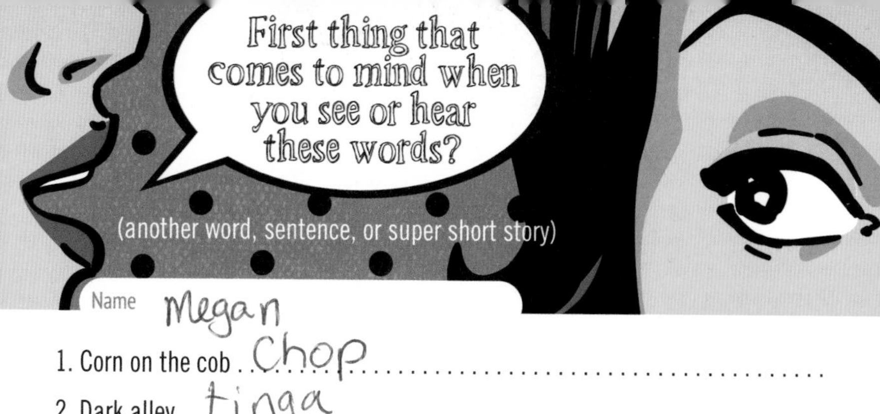

Name Megan

1. Corn on the cob . . Chop
2. Dark alley . . tinga
3. Roller coaster . . Woooo
4. Pigs in blankets . . but I love them♡
5. Hamster . . Run
6. Pink . . Just like fire!
7. Glow-in-the-dark . . Bracelet
8. The letter U . . Uranus
9. Hello Kitty . . bow
10. Face painting . . glitter
11. Super star . . bedazled microphone
12. Bell . . Cling
13. Sleeping bag . . Cold
14. Hollywood . . Famous
15. Rock . . chocolate pudding
16. Piano . . fingers
17. Magazine . . popular
18. Watermelon . . green
19. Bubbles . . america
20. Subway . . Sandwhich

classic

○ Waffle cone
○ Sugar cone
○ Cup?

○ Ice cubes
○ Crushed ice?

○ TV
○ Book?

○ Beach
○ Mountains?

○ Go with the flow
○ Stick to a routine?

○ Ice cream
○ Fro-yo?

Favorite relative?

Best amusement park ride?

Favorite game?

Best book?

coke-or-pepsi.com

last things i painted were my nails

1. Name

2. Best thing in a spray can? ○ Whipped Cream ○ Cheese Whiz ○ Paint

3. Ever sprayed whipped cream directly in your mouth? ○ Yes ○ No

4. Last thing you painted? ____________________

5. Last thing you had stuck in your hair? ____________________

6. ○ Donuts ○ Donut holes

7. Worse T-shirt color? ○ Orange ○ Yellow ○ Green

8. What are you a beginner at? ____________________

9. What are you an expert at? ____________________

10. Favorite dip? ____________________

11. Favorite thing to dip? ____________________

12. Scarves? ○ Luv 'em ○ Hate 'em, so restricting!

13. I heart ____________________.

14. ____________________ is epic.

15. Friend with the coolest family? ____________________

16. ○ Red velvet cheesecake brownie ○ S'more-stuffed chocolate chip cookie?

17. Fave flave for lipgloss? ____________________

18. Favorite emoticon? ____________________

19. ○ Abracadabra ○ Bipiddi-boppidi-boo ○ Expelliarmus?

20. ○ Lemonade ○ Pink Lemonade?

I like movies that make me cry

1. Name

2. Last animated movie you saw? ____________________

3. Movies ○ with happy endings ○ that leave you thinking?

4. Sleepovers? ○ Fun! ○ Ugh.

5. ○ French Bulldog ○ Irish Setter ○ Alaskan Husky?

6. **Movies ○ at the theater ○ at home?**

7. Are you a ○ share-your-umbrella ○ every-girl-for-herself kinda girl?

8. ○ Polo ○ Graphic Tee?

9. Love to see a ○ volcano erupt ○ total eclipse of the sun?

10. What does your hair do on rainy days? ____________________

11. **○ Write a great novel ○ Travel around the world?**

12. ○ Hike through the woods ○ Stroll through the city?

13. Ever danced the hula? ○ Yes ○ No

14. **Very first song you remember liking?** ____________________

15. Maple syrup on ○ waffles ○ French toast?

16. Ever fallen backwards in a chair? ○ Yes ○ No

17. **Wear shoes in the house? ○ Yes ○ Sometimes ○ Never**

18. If you get married, will you ○ keep ○ ditch ○ combine your last name(s)?

19. ○ Pack light ○ Certified overpacker?

20. FAVE SONG TO SING ON ROCK BAND OR GUITAR HERO? ____________________

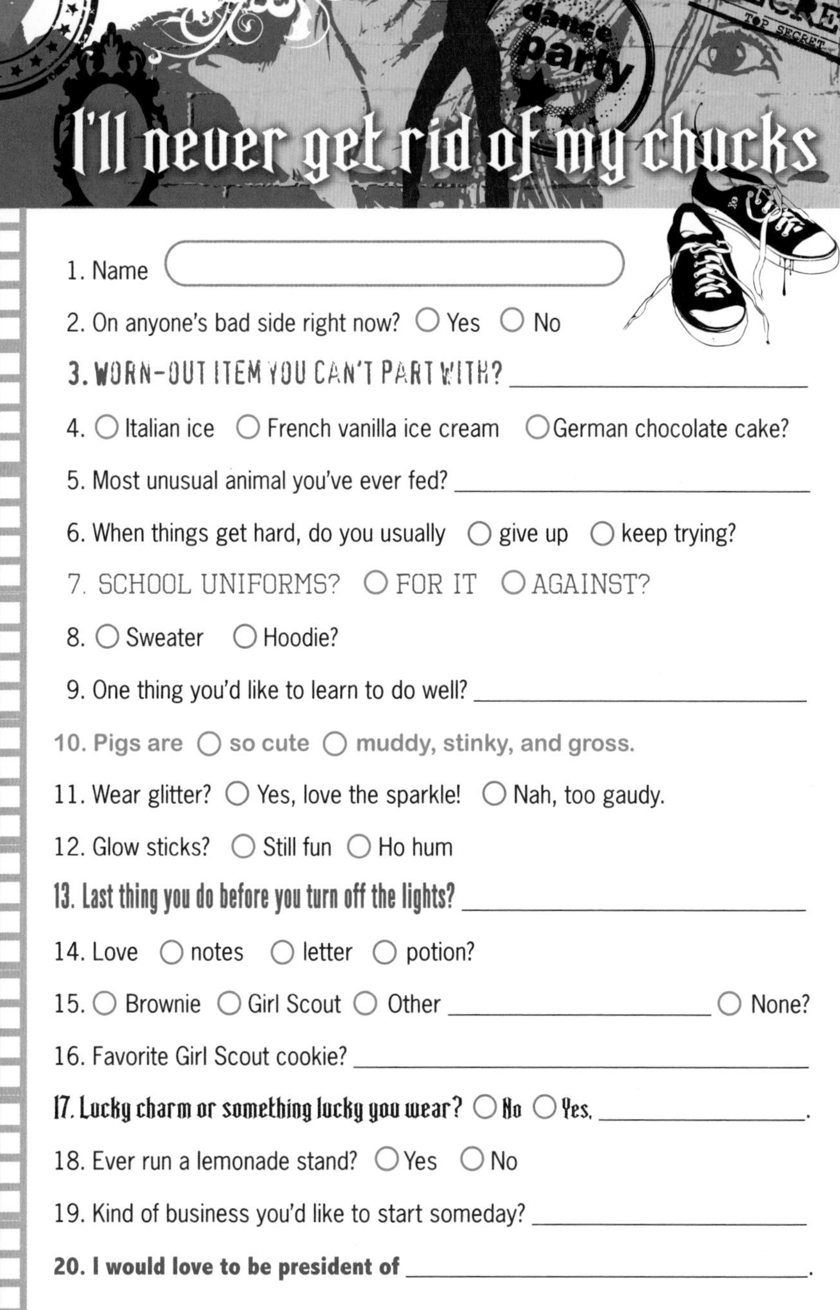

I'll never get rid of my chucks

1. Name

2. On anyone's bad side right now? ○ Yes ○ No

3. WORN-OUT ITEM YOU CAN'T PART WITH? ____________

4. ○ Italian ice ○ French vanilla ice cream ○ German chocolate cake?

5. Most unusual animal you've ever fed? ____________

6. When things get hard, do you usually ○ give up ○ keep trying?

7. SCHOOL UNIFORMS? ○ FOR IT ○ AGAINST?

8. ○ Sweater ○ Hoodie?

9. One thing you'd like to learn to do well? ____________

10. Pigs are ○ so cute ○ muddy, stinky, and gross.

11. Wear glitter? ○ Yes, love the sparkle! ○ Nah, too gaudy.

12. Glow sticks? ○ Still fun ○ Ho hum

13. Last thing you do before you turn off the lights? ____________

14. Love ○ notes ○ letter ○ potion?

15. ○ Brownie ○ Girl Scout ○ Other ____________ ○ None?

16. Favorite Girl Scout cookie? ____________

17. Lucky charm or something lucky you wear? ○ No ○ Yes, ____________.

18. Ever run a lemonade stand? ○ Yes ○ No

19. Kind of business you'd like to start someday? ____________

20. I would love to be president of ____________.

Twofers

Name

1. Fave sweet and salty combo?

2. Reasons for being late?

3. Things you always have with you?

4. Fave furry animals?

5. Habits you have?

6. Stuff outside your bedroom window?

7. Places you love?

8. Things you've climbed?

9. Words you really love?

10. Qualities you like in a friend?

11. Things that make you mad?

12. Fave animals that swim in the sea?

13. Green things you'll eat?

14. Black and white things you like?

15. Beverages you drink almost every day?

16. Things you love that fit in your hand?

17. Friends you talk to almost every day?

18. Colors you like to paint your toenails?

19. Stuff you've won?

20. Things you've lost?

1 question. 2 answers.

______________________________ forever.

____

____

______________________________ are so cute!

____

____

____

____

______________________________ are awesome words!

____

____

____

____

____

____

____

____

______________________________ are my favorites.

____

______________________________ are missing.

1. Name ( )

2. Leopard prints are so ○ chic ○ tacky?

3. ○ Seven dwarves ○ One fairy godmother?

4. How many tiaras do you own? ( )

5. Mannequins give you the creeps? ○ No ○ Yes

6. Ever been in a corn maze? ○ Yes ○ No ○ Not sure, what is that?

7. Last school project you did? ______________________

8. British accents sound ○ so cool ○ smart ○ kinda snobby?

9. ○ Pair of glass slippers ○ Pumpkin that turns into a carriage?

10. Magic ○ potion ○ wand ○ markers?

11. ○ Sand between your toes ○ Out too deep to touch bottom?

12. Bowling? ○ Ridiculous ○ Fun ○ Ridiculously fun!

13. What do you talk about more than anything? ______________________

14. Would you rather be a ○ princess ○ princess' sister?

15. Skinny jeans with ○ flats ○ flip-flops ○ sneakers?

16. Today are you ○ fairest of them all ○ "sleepy" beauty?

17. Three words to describe your life? ______________________

18. Favorite song to sing with friends? ______________________

19. How 'bout to dance to with friends? ______________________

20. I wish I were a(n) ○ English ○ history ○ math ○ science whiz!

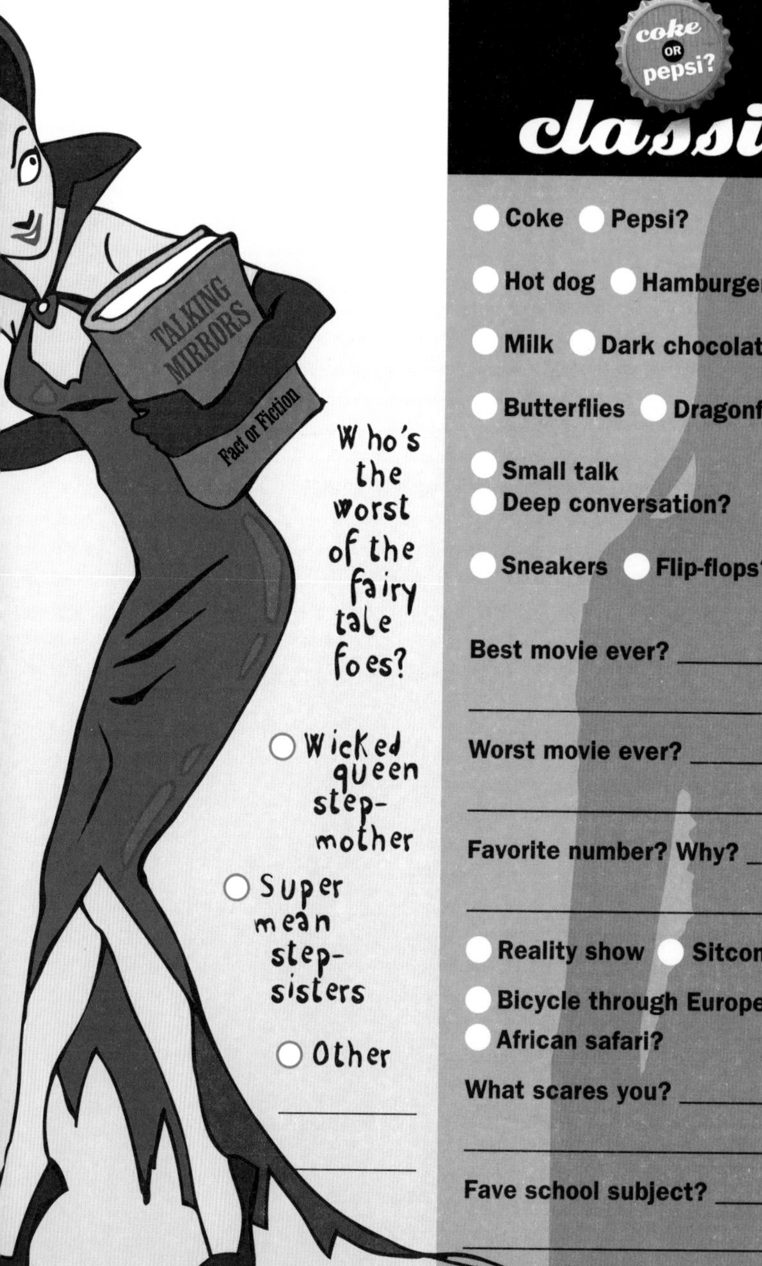

Who's the worst of the fairy tale foes?

- Wicked queen step-mother
- Super mean step-sisters
- Other ____________

____

coke OR pepsi?

classic

- Coke
- Pepsi?

- Hot dog
- Hamburger?

- Milk
- Dark chocolate?

- Butterflies
- Dragonflies?

- Small talk
- Deep conversation?

- Sneakers
- Flip-flops?

Best movie ever? ____________

____

Worst movie ever? ____________

____

Favorite number? Why? ____________

____

- Reality show
- Sitcom?

- Bicycle through Europe
- African safari?

What scares you? ____________

____

Fave school subject? ____________

____

I LOVE TWISTER!

1. Name ______

2. **Which have you taken a ride on?** ○ **Horse** ○ **Elephant** ○ **Camel** ○ **None!**

3. Team (s) you like to root for? ______

4. Favorite pasta topping? ○ Meatballs ○ Cheese ○ Other______

5. ○ Pencil ○ Pen ○ Keyboard?

6. **Own a pair of boots?** ○ **No** ○ **Yes,** ______ **pairs.**

7. How 'bout a cowboy hat? ○ Yep ○ No way

8. Like peanut butter? ○ No ○ Yes, ______ is my favorite kind.

9. Think quiet people are ○ smart ○ shy ○ not interested?

10. Ideal summer vacation? ______

11. Play a mean game of ping pong? ○ Yep, I'm awesome. ○ I'm OK. ○ No!

12. Last time you played Twister? ______

13. ○ Zoo ○ Aquarium ○ Neither, I like animals in the wild.

14. Do you like Scrabble? ○ Yes ○ No

15. Singer/Band that appears the most on your playlists? ______

16. ZOMBIES ARE CHASING YOU. WHO DO YOU WANT WITH YOU? ______

17. Huge sale at the mall. Who would you want with you? ______

18. Tried raw oysters? ○ No ○ Yes Did you like? ○ No! Ick! ○ Yes

19. Three things for a perfect weekend? ______

20. Own anything with polka dots on it? ○ Of course ○ Nope

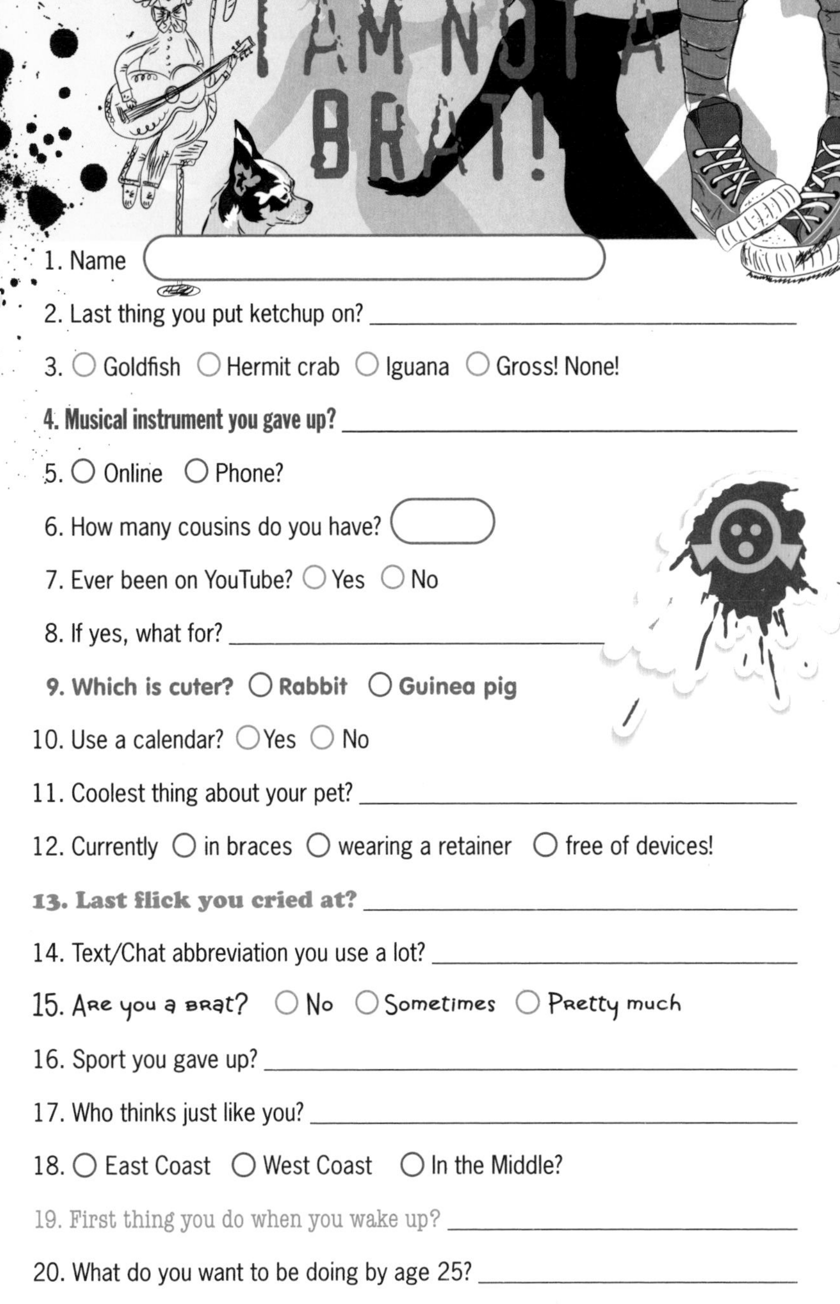

1. Name

2. Last thing you put ketchup on? ___

3. ○ Goldfish ○ Hermit crab ○ Iguana ○ Gross! None!

4. Musical instrument you gave up? ___

5. ○ Online ○ Phone?

6. How many cousins do you have?

7. Ever been on YouTube? ○ Yes ○ No

8. If yes, what for? ___

9. Which is cuter? ○ Rabbit ○ Guinea pig

10. Use a calendar? ○ Yes ○ No

11. Coolest thing about your pet? ___

12. Currently ○ in braces ○ wearing a retainer ○ free of devices!

13. Last flick you cried at? ___

14. Text/Chat abbreviation you use a lot? ___

15. Are you a brat? ○ No ○ Sometimes ○ Pretty much

16. Sport you gave up? ___

17. Who thinks just like you? ___

18. ○ East Coast ○ West Coast ○ In the Middle?

19. First thing you do when you wake up? ___

20. What do you want to be doing by age 25? ___

named that?

After megan fox

Mean

Do you like it?

☑ Yes   No ☐

Fave thing that comes in a wrapper?

wrap

Can you tie a good bow?

☐ Yes   No ☑

Would you rather ...

☐ Swim like a dolphin   ☑ Fly like an eagle?

Where would you swim to?

Where would you fly to?

frost valley

Do you interrrupt people?

☐ Yes ☹   ☐ No ☺

☐ Shake   ☐ Malt

What IS malt?

Fave flave?

oke-or-pepsi.com

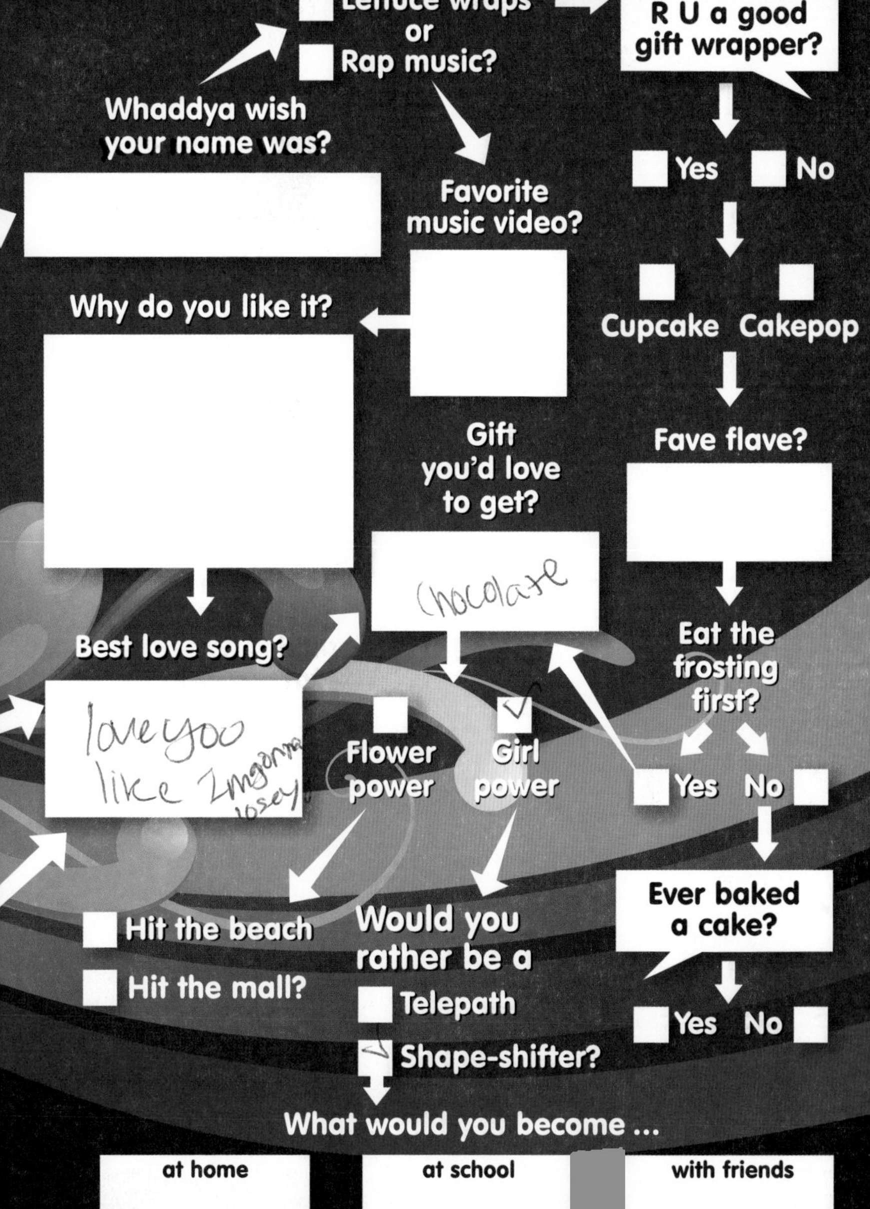

Lettuce wraps
or
Rap music?
R U a good
gift wrapper?
Yes
No
Whaddya wish
your name was?
Favorite
music video?
Cupcake
Cakepop
Why do you like it?
Fave flave?
Gift
you'd love
to get?
Chocolate
Best love song?
Eat the
frosting
first?
love you
like I'm gonna
losey
Flower
power
Girl
power
Yes
No
Ever baked
a cake?
Hit the beach
Hit the mall?
Would you
rather be a
Telepath
Shape-shifter?
Yes
No
What would you become ...
at home
at school
with friends

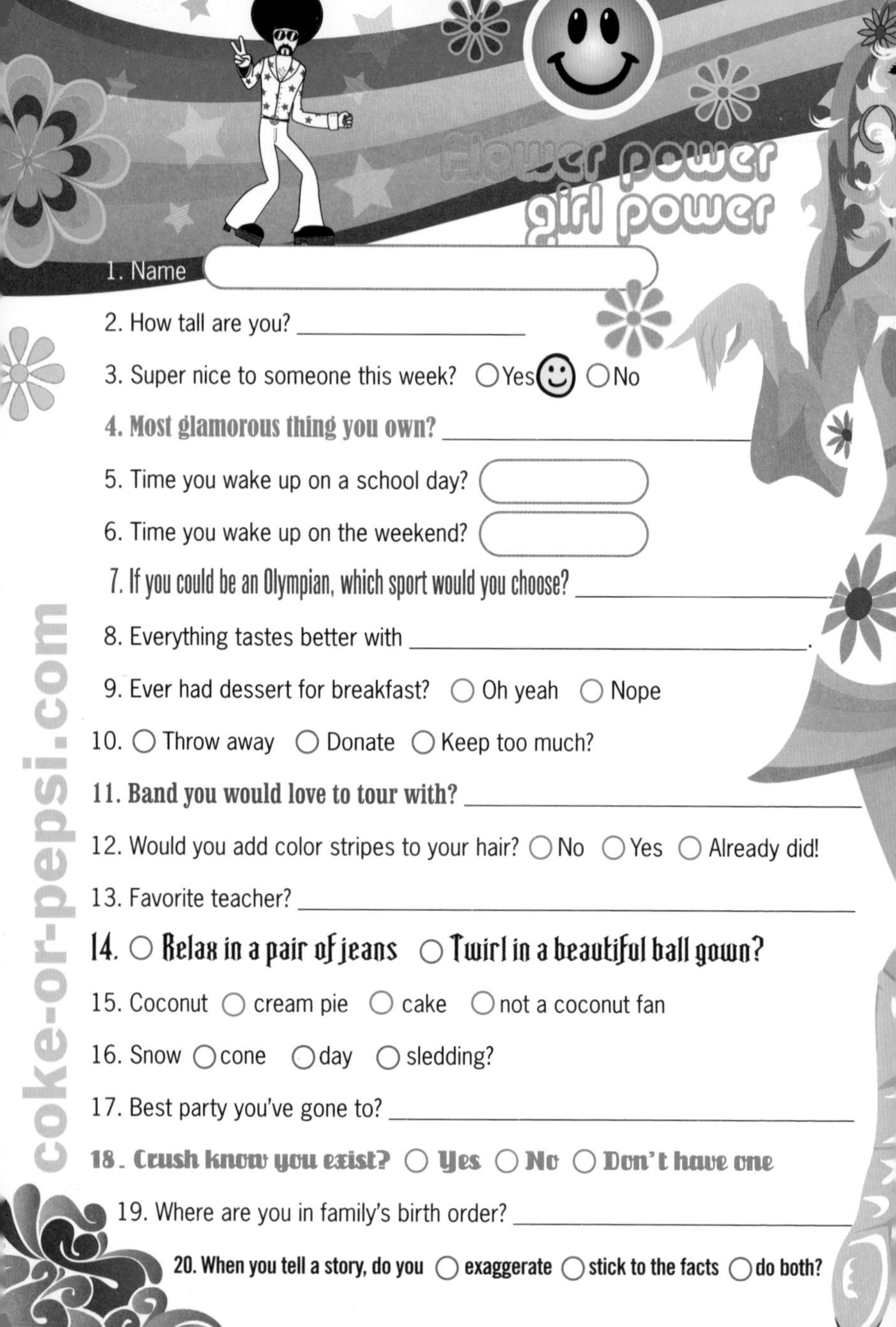

Flower power girl power

1. Name ____________________

2. How tall are you? ____________________

3. Super nice to someone this week? ○ Yes ○ No

4. **Most glamorous thing you own?** ____________________

5. Time you wake up on a school day? ____________________

6. Time you wake up on the weekend? ____________________

7. If you could be an Olympian, which sport would you choose? ____________________

8. Everything tastes better with ____________________.

9. Ever had dessert for breakfast? ○ Oh yeah ○ Nope

10. ○ Throw away ○ Donate ○ Keep too much?

11. **Band you would love to tour with?** ____________________

12. Would you add color stripes to your hair? ○ No ○ Yes ○ Already did!

13. Favorite teacher? ____________________

14. ○ Relax in a pair of jeans ○ Twirl in a beautiful ball gown?

15. Coconut ○ cream pie ○ cake ○ not a coconut fan

16. Snow ○ cone ○ day ○ sledding?

17. Best party you've gone to? ____________________

18. **Crush know you exist? ○ Yes ○ No ○ Don't have one**

19. Where are you in family's birth order? ____________________

20. **When you tell a story, do you ○ exaggerate ○ stick to the facts ○ do both?**

Peace Forever

1. Name

2. I'm wearing ○ lip gloss ○ nail polish ○ neither.

3. Which is worse? ○ Homework ○ Cleaning your room

4. How many pillows do you sleep with?

5. Favorite window to look out? ____________________

6. Something a parent does that drives you nuts? ____________________

7. Actress you would love to be a personal assistant to? ____________________

8. Are you more of a ○ pants ○ skirt girl?

9. If you could change one thing today, what would it be? ____________________

10. If you were an instrument, what would you be? ____________________

11. Best part of being a super heroine? ○ Power ○ Costume ○ Cool name

12. If you could only visit 1 Website this month, which would it be? ____________________

13. Best class trip ever? ____________________

14. Quality a friend has you wished you had? ____________________

15. One weird fact you know? ____________________

16. Coolest thing you've ever found? ____________________

17. Know anything about family ancestors? ○ No ○ Yes, ____________________.

18. Fave sleepover snacks? ____________________

19. Coordinate shoes and bag? ○ Always ○ Sometimes ○ Who cares?

20. If you had a safe, what would you keep in it? ____________________

1. **a mermaid,** where in the world would you want to live? Why?

____

2. **President,** what kind of room would you add to the White House?

____

3. an exotic **animal keeper,** which animals would you want to care for?

____

4. **in charge** of naming the next kind of American spacecraft, what awesome name would you give it? _______________________________

5. **a dog,** which neighborhood dogs would you want to hang with? Why?

____

6. **a teacher,** what cool activity would you do with your class?

____

7. **in charge of your school** for a day, what would you change?

____

8. **going to live** on the moon for one year who would you take with you? Why? _______________________________________

9. **able to stay** the same age for the rest of your life, which age would you pick? Why? ____________________________________

10. able to have any **talent** you don't currently have, what would it be?

____

First thing that comes to mind when you see or hear these words?

(another word, sentence, or super short story)

1. Panda bear . . . .
2. Hysterical . . . .
3. Fireworks . . . .
4. T-shirt . . . .
5. Marshmallow . . . .
6. Celery sticks . . . .
7. Raisins . . . .
8. Poodle . . . .
9. Sunglasses . . . .
10. Chucks . . . .
11. Stick people . . . .
12. Physical Education . . . .
13. Mountain . . . .
14. Scooter . . . .
15. Pyramid . . . .
16. Diamonds . . . .
17. Hot peppers . . . .
18. Ringtone . . . .
19. Nail polish . . . .
20. Alligator . . . .

Name

1. Name

2. ○ Cinnamon ○ Fruity ○ Minty gum?

3. What do you love about yourself? ____________

4. Where were you last time you used mustard? ____________

5. The last paper I wrote for a class was about ____________

____________.

6. I could never eat ____________ again and be OK.

7. TV show you most belong on? ____________

8. WOULD YOU RATHER BE THE ○ STAR ON A LOSING TEAM ○ WORST ON A STAR TEAM?

9. Ever carved anything in a tree? ○ Yes ○ No

10. ○ Swim with the dolphins ○ Pet a manatee?

11. Would you rather be a ○ giant ○ pixie?

12. ○ **Fuzzy socks** ○ **Warm slippers?**

13. Hot chocolate ○ with ○ without marshmallows?

14. Good at sneaking up on people? ○ Not really ○ Kind of ○ Absolutely!

15. Scariest thing you've done on purpose? ____________

16. New pair of ○ jeans ○ shoes?

17. **If I could ____________, I would be thrilled.**

18. Age you turned on fave birthday?

19. Something you would love to see? ____________

20. Which is worse? ○ Really sad ○ Out-of-control mad

Potato chips
French fries?
coke
OR
pepsi?
classic
Fashionable
Casual?
Sunset
Sunrise?
Brownies
Chocolate chip cookies?
Best holiday?
Fave actor?
Fave actress?
One word to describe you?
Big Mac
Whopper?
Gold
Silver?
coke-or-pepsi.com

orever

1. Name

2. ◯ Skinny jeans ◯ Jeggings ◯ Neither?

3. Happiest color? ______

4. What were you doing in the last photo taken of you? ______

5. Where were you? ______

6. Know how to cook? ◯ No ◯ A little ◯ Yes

7. If yes to #6, what's your specialty? ______

8. Are you usually ◯ cold ◯ hot?

9. Famous person you admire most? ______

10. DO HORROR MOVIES FRIGHTEN YOU? ◯ NOT REALLY ◯ YES, NIGHTMARES!

11. Fave outfit to relax in? ______

12. Ever shoot a spitball? ◯ Yes ◯ Gross, no!

13. Favorite thing that comes in your mail? ______.

14. Sprinkles ◯ always make me happy ◯ are kinda overrated.

15. Any phobias or fears? ◯ Nope ◯ Yes, I'm afraid of ______.

16. ◯ Drama queen ◯ Cool, calm, and collected?

17. What do you crave? ______

18. Drink after other people? ◯ Yeah ◯ Sometimes ◯ Never! Germs!

19. Ever encountered a bat? ◯ Yes ◯ No

20. What do you hear right now? ______

1. Name ______________________

2. Afraid to cross bridges? ○ Yes ○ No

3. Can you wiggle your ears without using your hands? ○ No ○ Yes

4. Do you ○ give in ○ get your way?

5. LAST THING YOU SOLD FOR YOUR SCHOOL? ______________________

6. Go to the library? ○ No ○ Yes

7. Longest word you know? ______________________

8. Can you hang a spoon from your nose? ○ Yes ○ No ○ Huh?

9. Best food with a glass of milk? ______________________

10. Gold ○ fish ○ bracelet?

11. Any strange talent? ○ No ○ Yes, I ______________________.

12. Spend the night in a haunted house? ○ NO! ○ Sure, I don't believe.

13. It's scary how much I like ______________________.

14. Give good manicures? ○ Yes ○ No

15. Favorite reality show? ______________________

16. Scrambled eggs are ○ yummy ○ frightening.

17. Worst thing about your brother(s)/sister(s)? ______________________

18. Best thing about your brother(s)/sister(s)? ______________________

19. LOVE A GOOD MYSTERY? ○ YES! ○ NAH

20. Think you're creative? ○ Yes ○ A little ○ Not really

Name

1. swim with a huge, harmless whale in the ocean, would you? ○Yes ○No, but I would swim with ______________________.

2. slow down time, which event would you slow down? ______________________

3. add sisters or brothers to your family, which genders and ages would you choose?

____

4. have absolutely anything for dinner tonight, what would you pick? ______________________

____

5. do one fun thing with an alien visiting our planet, what would it be? ______________________

____

6. become any object for just one day, what would you be? Why? ______________________

____

7. be an exchange student for one year anywhere in the world, which country would you visit? ______________________

8. be great friends with someone from the past, who would you choose? Why?

____

9. do absolutely anything for just one year, what would you do? ______________________

____

10. change your last name, without hurting your parents' feelings, would you?

○ No ○ Yes, I would change it to ______________________.

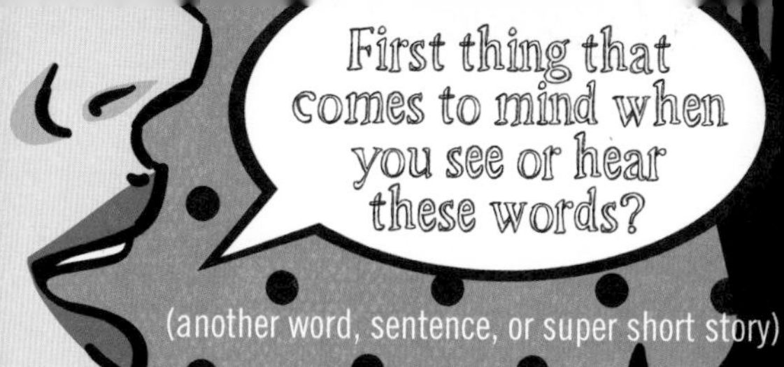

(another word, sentence, or super short story)

Name

1. Corn on the cob . . . .
2. Dark alley . . . .
3. Roller coaster . . . .
4. Pigs in blankets . . . .
5. Hamster . . . .
6. Pink . . . .
7. Glow-in-the-dark . . . .
8. The letter U . . . .
9. Hello Kitty . . . .
10. Face painting . . . .
11. Super star . . . .
12. Bell . . . .
13. Sleeping bag . . . .
14. Hollywood . . . .
15. Rock . . . .
16. Piano . . . .
17. Magazine . . . .
18. Watermelon . . . .
19. Bubbles . . . .
20. Subway . . . .

classic

- ◯ Waffle cone
- ◯ Sugar cone
- ◯ Cup?

- ◯ Ice cubes
- ◯ Crushed ice?

- ◯ TV
- ◯ Book?

- ◯ Beach
- ◯ Mountains?

- ◯ Go with the flow
- ◯ Stick to a routine?

- ◯ Ice cream
- ◯ Fro-yo?

Favorite relative?

Best amusement park ride?

Favorite game?

Best book?

last things i painted were my nails

1. Name

2. Best thing in a spray can? ○ Whipped Cream ○ Cheese Whiz ○ Paint

3. Ever sprayed whipped cream directly in your mouth? ○ Yes ○ No

4. Last thing you painted? ______

5. Last thing you had stuck in your hair? ______

6. ○ Donuts ○ Donut holes

7. Worse T-shirt color? ○ Orange ○ Yellow ○ Green

8. What are you a beginner at? ______

9. What are you an expert at? ______

10. Favorite dip? ______

11. Favorite thing to dip? ______

12. Scarves? ○ Luv 'em ○ Hate 'em, so restricting!

13. I heart ______.

14. ______ is epic.

15. Friend with the coolest family? ______

16. ○ Red velvet cheesecake brownie ○ S'more-stuffed chocolate chip cookie?

17. Fave flave for lipgloss? ______

18. Favorite emoticon? ______

19. ○ Abracadabra ○ Bipiddi-boppidi-boo ○ Expelliarmus?

20. ○ Lemonade ○ Pink Lemonade?

I like movies that make me cry

PRIVATE

1. Name

2. Last animated movie you saw? ____________________

3. Movies ◯ with happy endings ◯ that leave you thinking?

4. Sleepovers? ◯ Fun! ◯ Ugh.

5. ◯ French Bulldog ◯ Irish Setter ◯ Alaskan Husky?

6. **Movies ◯ at the theater ◯ at home?**

7. Are you a ◯ share-your-umbrella ◯ every-girl-for-herself kinda girl?

8. ◯ Polo ◯ Graphic Tee?

9. Love to see a ◯ volcano erupt ◯ total eclipse of the sun?

10. What does your hair do on rainy days? ____________________

11. **◯ Write a great novel ◯ Travel around the world?**

12. ◯ Hike through the woods ◯ Stroll through the city?

13. Ever danced the hula? ◯ Yes ◯ No

14. **Very first song you remember liking?** ____________________

15. Maple syrup on ◯ waffles ◯ French toast?

16. Ever fallen backwards in a chair? ◯ Yes ◯ No

17. **Wear shoes in the house? ◯ Yes ◯ Sometimes ◯ Never**

18. If you get married, will you ◯ keep ◯ ditch ◯ combine your last name(s)?

19. ◯ Pack light ◯ Certified overpacker?

20. FAVE SONG TO SING ON ROCK BAND OR GUITAR HERO? ____________________

I'll never get rid of my chucks

1. Name

2. On anyone's bad side right now? ○ Yes ○ No

3. WORN-OUT ITEM YOU CAN'T PART WITH? ______________

4. ○ Italian ice ○ French vanilla ice cream ○ German chocolate cake?

5. Most unusual animal you've ever fed? ______________

6. When things get hard, do you usually ○ give up ○ keep trying?

7. SCHOOL UNIFORMS? ○ FOR IT ○ AGAINST?

8. ○ Sweater ○ Hoodie?

9. One thing you'd like to learn to do well? ______________

10. Pigs are ○ so cute ○ muddy, stinky, and gross.

11. Wear glitter? ○ Yes, love the sparkle! ○ Nah, too gaudy.

12. Glow sticks? ○ Still fun ○ Ho hum

13. Last thing you do before you turn off the lights? ______________

14. Love ○ notes ○ letter ○ potion?

15. ○ Brownie ○ Girl Scout ○ Other ______________ ○ None?

16. Favorite Girl Scout cookie? ______________

17. Lucky charm or something lucky you wear? ○ No ○ Yes, ______________.

18. Ever run a lemonade stand? ○ Yes ○ No

19. Kind of business you'd like to start someday? ______________

20. I would love to be president of ______________.

Name

1. Fave sweet and salty combo?

2. Reasons for being late?

3. Things you always have with you?

4. Fave furry animals?

5. Habits you have?

6. Stuff outside your bedroom window?

7. Places you love?

8. Things you've climbed?

9. Words you really love?

10. Qualities you like in a friend?

11. Things that make you mad?

12. Fave animals that swim in the sea?

13. Green things you'll eat?

14. Black and white things you like?

15. Beverages you drink almost every day?

16. Things you love that fit in your hand?

17. Friends you talk to almost every day?

18. Colors you like to paint your toenails?

19. Stuff you've won?

20. Things you've lost?

1 question. 2 answers.

forever.

are so cute!

are awesome words!

are my favorites.

are missing.

1. Name

2. Leopard prints are so ○ chic ○ tacky?

3. ○ Seven dwarves ○ One fairy godmother?

4. How many tiaras do you own?

5. Mannequins give you the creeps? ○ No ○ Yes

6. Ever been in a corn maze? ○ Yes ○ No ○ Not sure, what is that?

7. Last school project you did? ______

8. British accents sound ○ so cool ○ smart ○ kinda snobby?

9. ○ Pair of glass slippers ○ Pumpkin that turns into a carriage?

10. Magic ○ potion ○ wand ○ markers?

11. ○ Sand between your toes ○ Out too deep to touch bottom?

12. Bowling? ○ Ridiculous ○ Fun ○ Ridiculously fun!

13. What do you talk about more than anything? ______

14. Would you rather be a ○ princess ○ princess' sister?

15. Skinny jeans with ○ flats ○ flip-flops ○ sneakers?

16. Today are you ○ fairest of them all ○ "sleepy" beauty?

17. Three words to describe your life? ______

18. Favorite song to sing with friends? ______

19. How 'bout to dance to with friends? ______

20. I wish I were a(n) ○ English ○ history ○ math ○ science whiz!

Who's the worst of the fairy tale foes?

- Wicked queen step-mother
- Super mean step-sisters
- Other

____

____

coke OR pepsi?

classic

- Coke - Pepsi?
- Hot dog - Hamburger?
- Milk - Dark chocolate?
- Butterflies - Dragonflies?
- Small talk
- Deep conversation?
- Sneakers - Flip-flops?

Best movie ever? ________

____

Worst movie ever? ________

____

Favorite number? Why? ________

____

- Reality show - Sitcom?
- Bicycle through Europe
- African safari?

What scares you? ________

____

Fave school subject? ________

____

I LOVE TWISTER!

1. Name

2. Which have you taken a ride on? ○ Horse ○ Elephant ○ Camel ○ None!

3. Team(s) you like to root for? ____

4. Favorite pasta topping? ○ Meatballs ○ Cheese ○ Other____

5. ○ Pencil ○ Pen ○ Keyboard?

6. Own a pair of boots? ○ No ○ Yes, ____ pairs.

7. How 'bout a cowboy hat? ○ Yep ○ No way

8. Like peanut butter? ○ No ○ Yes, ____ is my favorite kind.

9. Think quiet people are ○ smart ○ shy ○ not interested?

10. Ideal summer vacation? ____

11. Play a mean game of ping pong? ○ Yep, I'm awesome. ○ I'm OK. ○ No!

12. Last time you played Twister? ____

13. ○ Zoo ○ Aquarium ○ Neither, I like animals in the wild.

14. Do you like Scrabble? ○ Yes ○ No

15. Singer/Band that appears the most on your playlists? ____

16. ZOMBIES ARE CHASING YOU. WHO DO YOU WANT WITH YOU? ____

17. Huge sale at the mall. Who would you want with you? ____

18. Tried raw oysters? ○ No ○ Yes Did you like? ○ No! Ick! ○ Yes

19. Three things for a perfect weekend? ____

20. Own anything with polka dots on it? ○ Of course ○ Nope

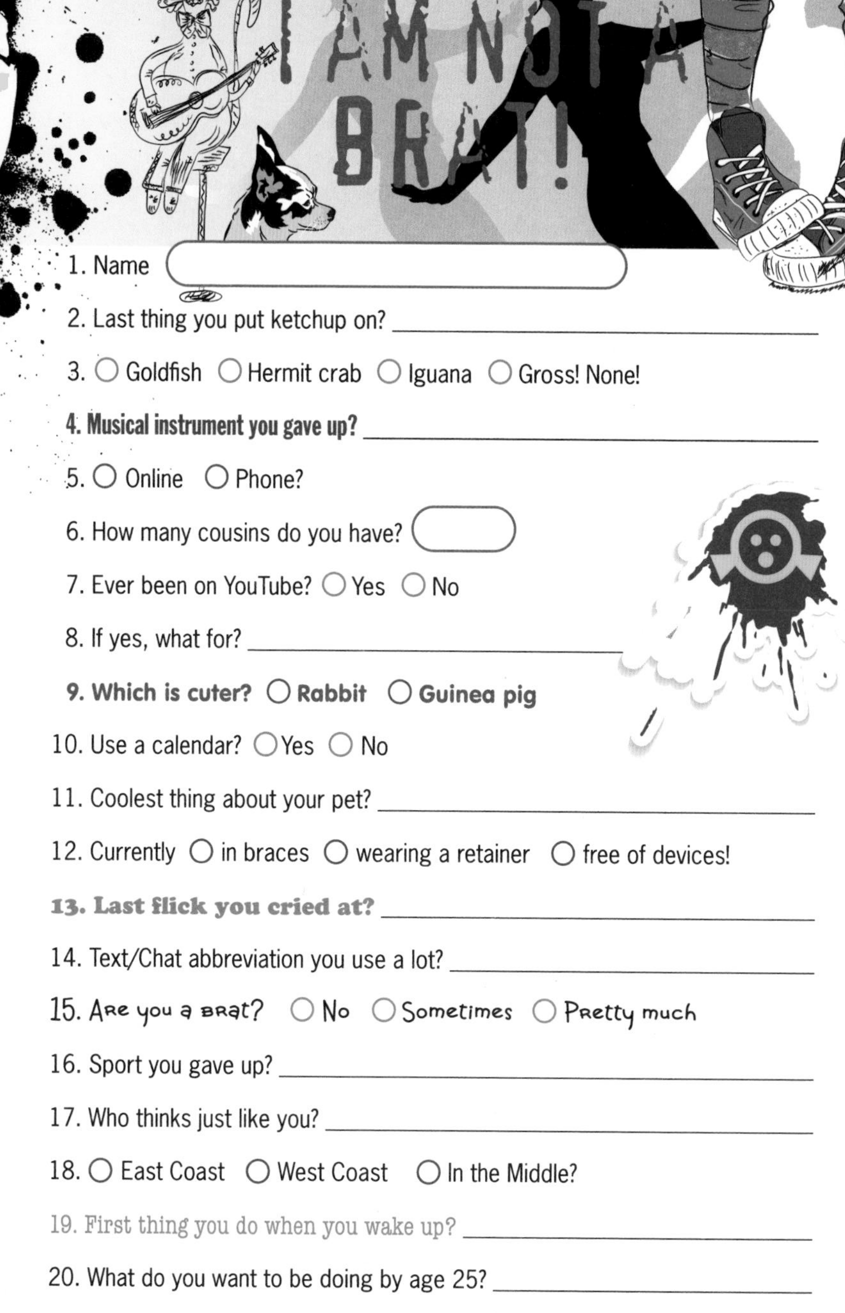

I AM NOT A BRAT!

1. Name

2. Last thing you put ketchup on? ______

3. ○ Goldfish ○ Hermit crab ○ Iguana ○ Gross! None!

4. Musical instrument you gave up? ______

5. ○ Online ○ Phone?

6. How many cousins do you have?

7. Ever been on YouTube? ○ Yes ○ No

8. If yes, what for? ______

9. Which is cuter? ○ Rabbit ○ Guinea pig

10. Use a calendar? ○ Yes ○ No

11. Coolest thing about your pet? ______

12. Currently ○ in braces ○ wearing a retainer ○ free of devices!

13. Last flick you cried at? ______

14. Text/Chat abbreviation you use a lot? ______

15. Are you a brat? ○ No ○ Sometimes ○ Pretty much

16. Sport you gave up? ______

17. Who thinks just like you? ______

18. ○ East Coast ○ West Coast ○ In the Middle?

19. First thing you do when you wake up? ______

20. What do you want to be doing by age 25? ______

named that?

Fave thing that comes in a wrapper?

Can you tie a good bow?

Yes

No

Do you interrrupt people?

Yes ☹

No ☺

Shake

Malt

Fave flave?

Do you like it?

Yes

No

Would you rather ...

Swim like a dolphin

Fly like an eagle?

Where would you swim to?

Where would you fly to?

What IS malt?

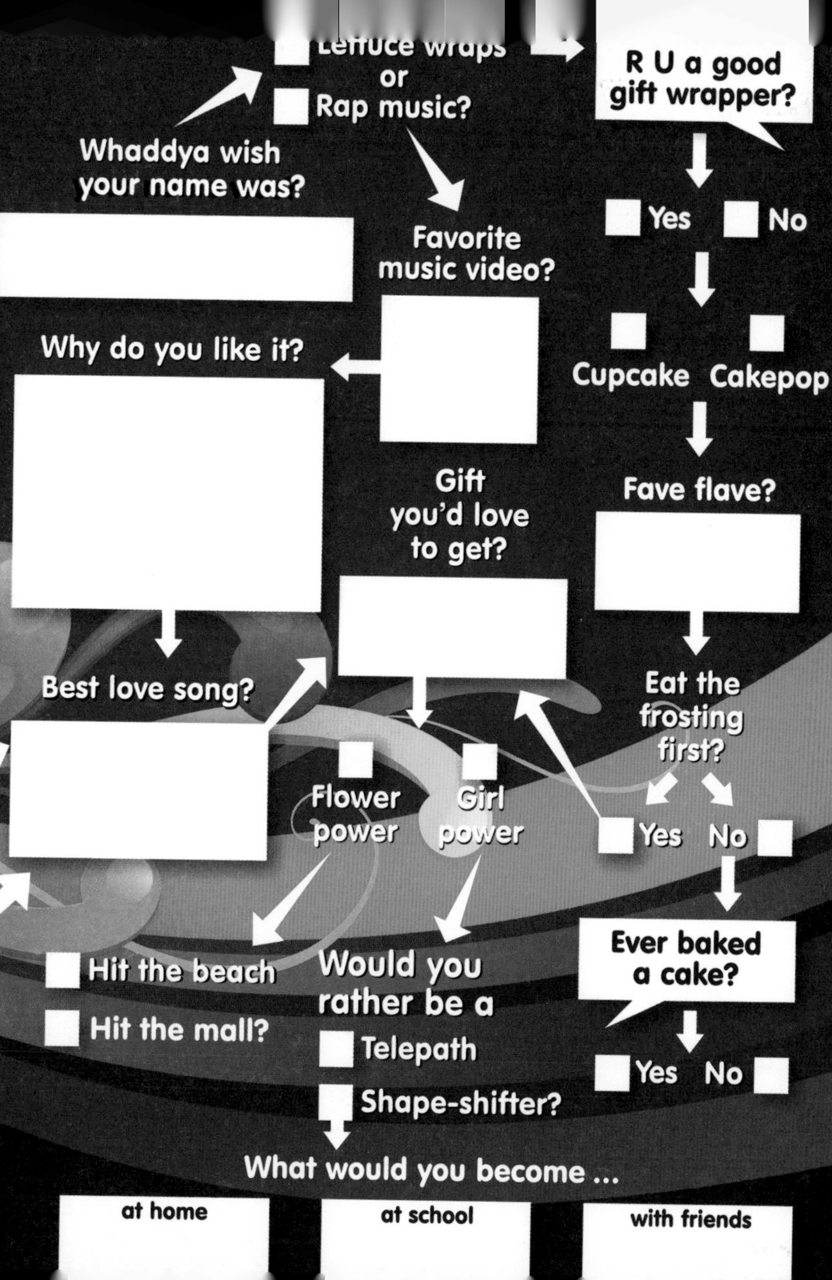
Lettuce wraps
or
Rap music?
R U a good gift wrapper?
Yes
No
Whaddya wish your name was?
Favorite music video?
Cupcake
Cakepop
Why do you like it?
Gift you'd love to get?
Fave flave?
Best love song?
Eat the frosting first?
Flower power
Girl power
Yes
No
Ever baked a cake?
Hit the beach
Hit the mall?
Would you rather be a
Telepath
Shape-shifter?
Yes
No
What would you become ...
at home
at school
with friends

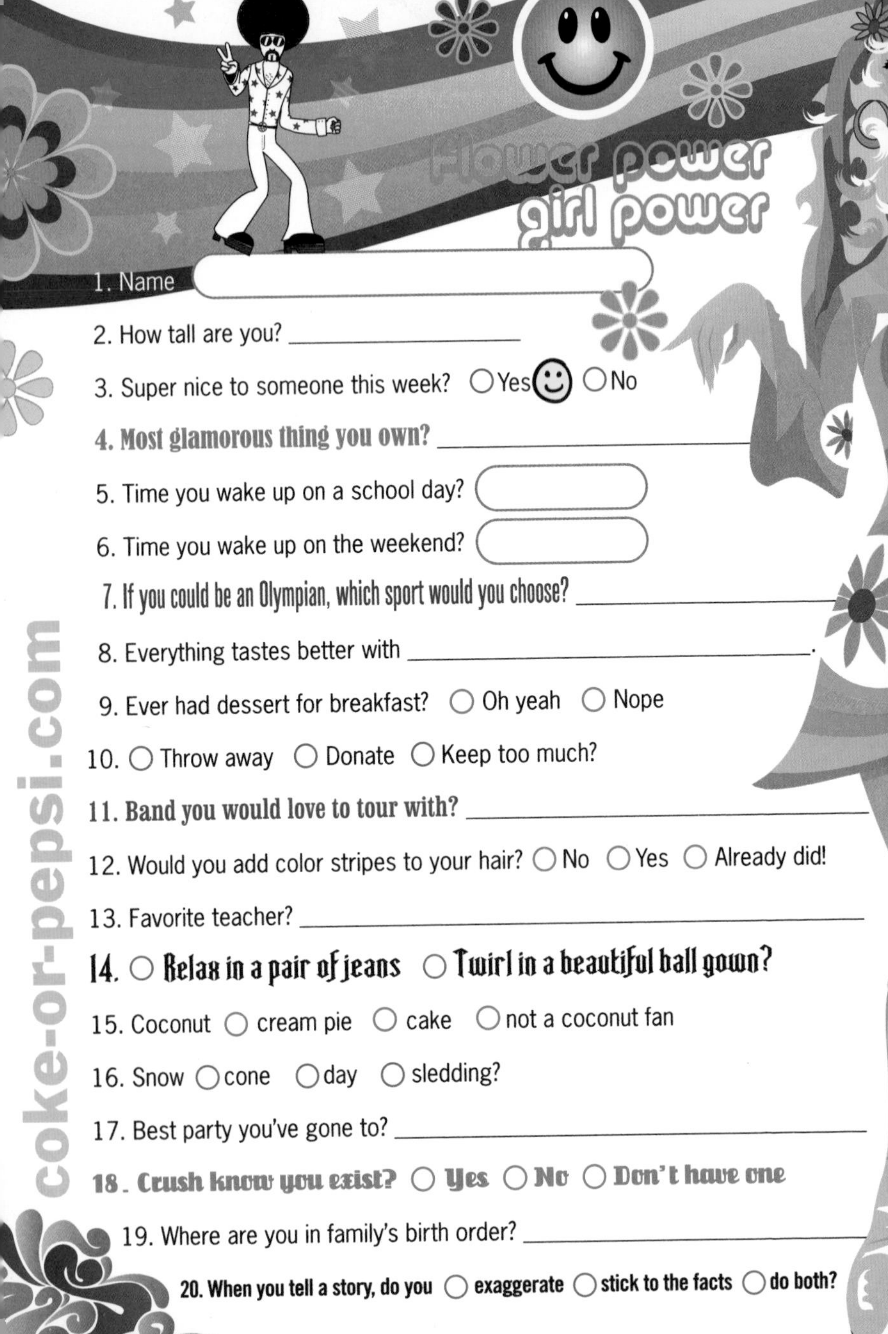

1. Name

2. How tall are you? ______

3. Super nice to someone this week? ○ Yes ○ No

4. Most glamorous thing you own? ______

5. Time you wake up on a school day?

6. Time you wake up on the weekend?

7. If you could be an Olympian, which sport would you choose? ______

8. Everything tastes better with ______.

9. Ever had dessert for breakfast? ○ Oh yeah ○ Nope

10. ○ Throw away ○ Donate ○ Keep too much?

11. Band you would love to tour with? ______

12. Would you add color stripes to your hair? ○ No ○ Yes ○ Already did!

13. Favorite teacher? ______

14. ○ Relax in a pair of jeans ○ Twirl in a beautiful ball gown?

15. Coconut ○ cream pie ○ cake ○ not a coconut fan

16. Snow ○ cone ○ day ○ sledding?

17. Best party you've gone to? ______

18. Crush know you exist? ○ Yes ○ No ○ Don't have one

19. Where are you in family's birth order? ______

20. When you tell a story, do you ○ exaggerate ○ stick to the facts ○ do both?

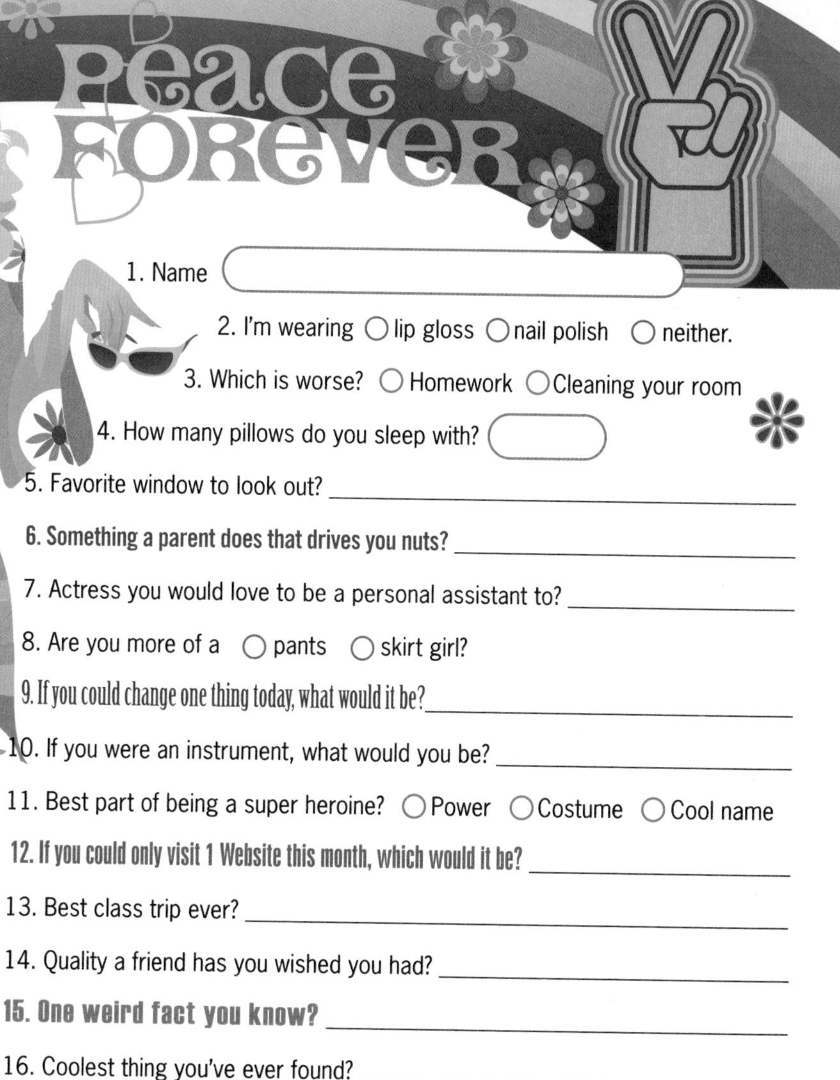

1. Name

2. I'm wearing ○ lip gloss ○ nail polish ○ neither.

3. Which is worse? ○ Homework ○ Cleaning your room

4. How many pillows do you sleep with?

5. Favorite window to look out? ______

6. Something a parent does that drives you nuts? ______

7. Actress you would love to be a personal assistant to? ______

8. Are you more of a ○ pants ○ skirt girl?

9. If you could change one thing today, what would it be? ______

10. If you were an instrument, what would you be? ______

11. Best part of being a super heroine? ○ Power ○ Costume ○ Cool name

12. If you could only visit 1 Website this month, which would it be? ______

13. Best class trip ever? ______

14. Quality a friend has you wished you had? ______

15. One weird fact you know? ______

16. Coolest thing you've ever found? ______

17. Know anything about family ancestors? ○ No ○ Yes, ______.

18. Fave sleepover snacks? ______

19. Coordinate shoes and bag? ○ Always ○ Sometimes ○ Who cares?

20. If you had a safe, what would you keep in it? ______

If you were ...

Name

1. **a mermaid,** where in the world would you want to live? Why?

______

2. **President,** what kind of room would you add to the White House?

______

3. an exotic **animal keeper,** which animals would you want to care for?

______

4. **in charge** of naming the next kind of American spacecraft, what awesome name would you give it? ______

5. **a dog,** which neighborhood dogs would you want to hang with? Why?

______

6. **a teacher,** what cool activity would you do with your class?

______

7. **in charge of your school** for a day, what would you change?

______

8. **going to live** on the moon for one year who would you take with you? Why? ______

9. **able to stay** the same age for the rest of your life, which age would you pick? Why? ______

10. able to have any **talent** you don't currently have, what would it be?

______

First thing that comes to mind when you see or hear these words?

(another word, sentence, or super short story)

1. Panda bear .... panda the song
2. Hysterical .... noemi
3. Fireworks .... 7th of July
4. T-shirt .... Knols commercial
5. Marshmallow .... smores
6. Celery sticks .... Martin
7. Raisins .... noemi
8. Poodle ....
9. Sunglasses ....
10. Chucks ....
11. Stick people ....
12. Physical Education ....
13. Mountain ....
14. Scooter ....
15. Pyramid ....
16. Diamonds ....
17. Hot peppers ....
18. Ringtone ....
19. Nail polish ....
20. Alligator ....

Name

1. Name Jessica [illegible]

2. ○ Cinnamon ○ Fruity ✓ Minty gum?

3. What do you love about yourself? Sense of humor

4. Where were you last time you used mustard? In my house

5. The last paper I wrote for a class was about The nab awards.

6. I could never eat chicken on a bone again and be OK.

7. TV show you most belong on? Suvivor

8. WOULD YOU RATHER BE THE ○ STAR ON A LOSING TEAM ○ WORST ON A STAR TEAM?

9. Ever carved anything in a tree? ● Yes ○ No

10. ● Swim with the dolphins ○ Pet a manatee?

11. Would you rather be a ○ giant ● pixie?

12. ○ Fuzzy socks ● Warm slippers?

13. Hot chocolate ○ with ● without marshmallows?

14. Good at sneaking up on people? ○ Not really ○ Kind of ● Absolutely!

15. Scariest thing you've done on purpose? gone into a ocean with big wave

16. New pair of ● jeans ○ shoes?

17. If I could do an ironman, I would be thrilled.

18. Age you turned on fave birthday? 30

19. Something you would love to see? Marin be happy

20. Which is worse? ○ Really sad ● Out-of-control mad

Potato chips
French fries?
coke
OR
pepsi?
classic
Fashionable
Casual?
Sunset
Sunrise?
Brownies
Chocolate chip cookies?
Best holiday?
Fave actor?
Fave actress?
One word to describe you?
Big Mac
Whopper?
Gold
Silver?
coke-or-pepsi.com

orever

1. Name

2. ◯ Skinny jeans ◯ Jeggings ◯ Neither?

3. Happiest color? ______

4. What were you doing in the last photo taken of you? ______

5. Where were you? ______

6. Know how to cook? ◯ **No** ◯ **A little** ◯ **Yes**

7. If yes to #6, what's your specialty? ______

8. Are you usually ◯ cold ◯ hot?

9. Famous person you admire most? ______

10. DO HORROR MOVIES FRIGHTEN YOU? ◯ **NOT REALLY** ◯ **YES, NIGHTMARES!**

11. Fave outfit to relax in? ______

12. Ever shoot a spitball? ◯ Yes ◯ Gross, no!

13. Favorite thing that comes in your mail? ______.

14. Sprinkles ◯ always make me happy ◯ are kinda overrated.

15. Any phobias or fears? ◯ Nope ◯ Yes, I'm afraid of ______.

16. ◯ Drama queen ◯ Cool, calm, and collected?

17. What do you crave? ______

18. Drink after other people? ◯ Yeah ◯ Sometimes ◯ Never! Germs!

19. Ever encountered a bat? ◯ Yes ◯ No

20. What do you hear right now? ______

EAR

Ahh! You're going to wear that?

Scare-crow! Caww!

1. Name

2. Afraid to cross bridges? ◯ Yes ◯ No

3. Can you wiggle your ears without using your hands? ◯ No ◯ Yes

4. Do you ◯ give in ◯ get your way?

5. LAST THING YOU SOLD FOR YOUR SCHOOL? ______________________

6. Go to the library? ◯ No ◯ Yes

7. Longest word you know? ______________________

8. Can you hang a spoon from your nose? ◯ Yes ◯ No ◯ Huh?

9. Best food with a glass of milk? ______________________

10. Gold ◯ fish ◯ bracelet?

11. Any strange talent? ◯ No ◯ Yes, I ______________________.

12. Spend the night in a haunted house? ◯ NO! ◯ Sure, I don't believe.

13. It's scary how much I like ______________________.

14. Give good manicures? ◯ Yes ◯ No

15. Favorite reality show? ______________________

16. Scrambled eggs are ◯ yummy ◯ frightening.

17. Worst thing about your brother(s)/sister(s)? ______________________

18. Best thing about your brother(s)/sister(s)? ______________________

19. LOVE A GOOD MYSTERY? ◯ YES! ◯ NAH

20. Think you're creative? ◯ Yes ◯ A little ◯ Not really

Name

1. swim with a huge, harmless whale in the ocean, would you? ○Yes ○No, but I would swim with ______________________________.

2. slow down time, which event would you slow down? ______________________

3. add sisters or brothers to your family, which genders and ages would you choose?

____

4. have absolutely anything for dinner tonight, what would you pick? ___________

____

5. do one fun thing with an alien visiting our planet, what would it be? _________

____

6. become any object for just one day, what would you be? Why? _____________

____

7. be an exchange student for one year anywhere in the world, which country would you visit? ______________________________

8. be great friends with someone from the past, who would you choose? Why?

____

9. do absolutely anything for just one year, what would you do? _____________

____

10. change your last name, without hurting your parents' feelings, would you?

○ No ○ Yes, I would change it to ______________________.

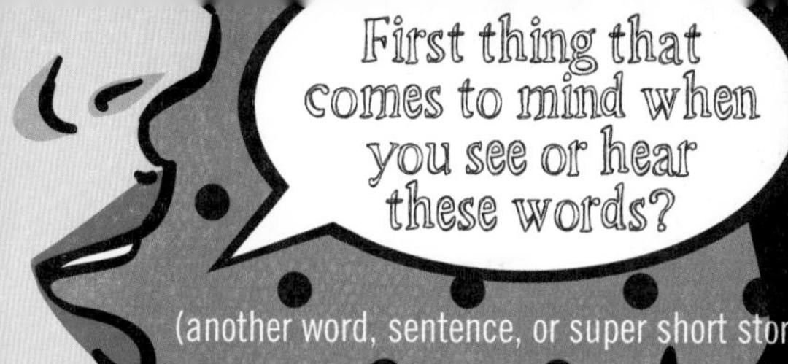

(another word, sentence, or super short story)

Name

1. Corn on the cob . . . .
2. Dark alley . . . .
3. Roller coaster . . . .
4. Pigs in blankets . . . .
5. Hamster . . . .
6. Pink . . . .
7. Glow-in-the-dark . . . .
8. The letter U . . . .
9. Hello Kitty . . . .
10. Face painting . . . .
11. Super star . . . .
12. Bell . . . .
13. Sleeping bag . . . .
14. Hollywood . . . .
15. Rock . . . .
16. Piano . . . .
17. Magazine . . . .
18. Watermelon . . . .
19. Bubbles . . . .
20. Subway . . . .

coke or pepsi?

classic

- ◯ Waffle cone
- ◯ Sugar cone
- ◯ Cup?

- ◯ Ice cubes
- ◯ Crushed ice?

- ◯ TV
- ◯ Book?

- ◯ Beach
- ◯ Mountains?

- ◯ Go with the flow
- ◯ Stick to a routine?

- ◯ Ice cream
- ◯ Fro-yo?

Favorite relative?

Best amusement park ride?

Favorite game?

Best book?

last things i painted were my nails

1. Name ____________

2. Best thing in a spray can? ○ Whipped Cream ○ Cheese Whiz ○ Paint

3. Ever sprayed whipped cream directly in your mouth? ○ Yes ○ No

4. Last thing you painted? ____________

5. Last thing you had stuck in your hair? ____________

6. ○ Donuts ○ Donut holes

7. **Worse T-shirt color?** ○ **Orange** ○ **Yellow** ○ **Green**

8. What are you a beginner at? ____________

9. What are you an expert at? ____________

10. **Favorite dip?** ____________

11. Favorite thing to dip? ____________

12. Scarves? ○ Luv 'em ○ Hate 'em, so restricting!

13. I heart ____________.

14. ____________ is epic.

15. Friend with the coolest family? ____________

16. ○ Red velvet cheesecake brownie ○ S'more-stuffed chocolate chip cookie?

17. Fave flave for lipgloss? ____________

18. Favorite emoticon? ____________

19. ○ Abracadabra ○ Bipiddi-boppidi-boo ○ Expelliarmus?

20. ○ Lemonade ○ Pink Lemonade?

PRIVATE

I like movies that make me cry

1. Name

2. Last animated movie you saw? ______

3. Movies ○ with happy endings ○ that leave you thinking?

4. Sleepovers? ○ Fun! ○ Ugh.

5. ○ French Bulldog ○ Irish Setter ○ Alaskan Husky?

6. **Movies ○ at the theater ○ at home?**

7. Are you a ○ share-your-umbrella ○ every-girl-for-herself kinda girl?

8. ○ Polo ○ Graphic Tee?

9. Love to see a ○ volcano erupt ○ total eclipse of the sun?

10. What does your hair do on rainy days? ______

11. **○ Write a great novel ○ Travel around the world?**

12. ○ Hike through the woods ○ Stroll through the city?

13. Ever danced the hula? ○ Yes ○ No

14. **Very first song you remember liking?** ______

15. Maple syrup on ○ waffles ○ French toast?

16. Ever fallen backwards in a chair? ○ Yes ○ No

17. **Wear shoes in the house? ○ Yes ○ Sometimes ○ Never**

18. If you get married, will you ○ keep ○ ditch ○ combine your last name(s)?

19. ○ Pack light ○ Certified overpacker?

20. FAVE SONG TO SING ON ROCK BAND OR GUITAR HERO? ______

I'll never get rid of my chucks

1. Name ____________________
2. On anyone's bad side right now? ○ Yes ○ No
3. WORN-OUT ITEM YOU CAN'T PART WITH? ____________________
4. ○ Italian ice ○ French vanilla ice cream ○ German chocolate cake?
5. Most unusual animal you've ever fed? ____________________
6. When things get hard, do you usually ○ give up ○ keep trying?
7. SCHOOL UNIFORMS? ○ FOR IT ○ AGAINST?
8. ○ Sweater ○ Hoodie?
9. One thing you'd like to learn to do well? ____________________
10. Pigs are ○ so cute ○ muddy, stinky, and gross.
11. Wear glitter? ○ Yes, love the sparkle! ○ Nah, too gaudy.
12. Glow sticks? ○ Still fun ○ Ho hum
13. Last thing you do before you turn off the lights? ____________________
14. Love ○ notes ○ letter ○ potion?
15. ○ Brownie ○ Girl Scout ○ Other ____________________ ○ None?
16. Favorite Girl Scout cookie? ____________________
17. Lucky charm or something lucky you wear? ○ No ○ Yes, ____________________.
18. Ever run a lemonade stand? ○ Yes ○ No
19. Kind of business you'd like to start someday? ____________________
20. I would love to be president of ____________________.

Name ______________________

1. Fave sweet and salty combo? ______________________

2. Reasons for being late? ______________________

3. Things you always have with you? ______________________

4. Fave furry animals? ______________________

5. Habits you have? ______________________

6. Stuff outside your bedroom window? ______________________

7. Places you love? ______________________

8. Things you've climbed? ______________________

9. Words you really love? ______________________

10. Qualities you like in a friend? ______________________

11. Things that make you mad? ______________________

12. Fave animals that swim in the sea? ______________________

13. Green things you'll eat? ______________________

14. Black and white things you like? ______________________

15. Beverages you drink almost every day? ______________________

16. Things you love that fit in your hand? ______________________

17. Friends you talk to almost every day? ______________________

18. Colors you like to paint your toenails? ______________________

19. Stuff you've won? ______________________

20. Things you've lost? ______________________

1 question. 2 answers.

______ forever.

______

______

______ are so cute!

______

______

______

______

______ are awesome words!

______

______

______

______

______

______

______

______ are my favorites.

______

______ are missing.

1. Name

2. Leopard prints are so ○ chic ○ tacky?

3. ○ Seven dwarves ○ One fairy godmother?

4. How many tiaras do you own?

5. Mannequins give you the creeps? ○ No ○ Yes

6. Ever been in a corn maze? ○ Yes ○ No ○ Not sure, what is that?

7. Last school project you did? ____________________

8. British accents sound ○ so cool ○ smart ○ kinda snobby?

9. ○ Pair of glass slippers ○ Pumpkin that turns into a carriage?

10. Magic ○ potion ○ wand ○ markers?

11. ○ Sand between your toes ○ Out too deep to touch bottom?

12. Bowling? ○ Ridiculous ○ Fun ○ Ridiculously fun!

13. What do you talk about more than anything? ____________________

14. Would you rather be a ○ princess ○ princess' sister?

15. Skinny jeans with ○ flats ○ flip-flops ○ sneakers?

16. Today are you ○ fairest of them all ○ "sleepy" beauty?

17. Three words to describe your life? ____________________

18. Favorite song to sing with friends? ____________________

19. How 'bout to dance to with friends? ____________________

20. I wish I were a(n) ○ English ○ history ○ math ○ science whiz!

coke OR pepsi?

classic

- Coke ○ Pepsi?
- ○ Hot dog ○ Hamburger?
- ○ Milk ○ Dark chocolate?
- ○ Butterflies ○ Dragonflies?
- ○ Small talk ○ Deep conversation?
- ○ Sneakers ○ Flip-flops?

Best movie ever? ______

Worst movie ever? ______

Favorite number? Why? ______

- ○ Reality show ○ Sitcom?
- ○ Bicycle through Europe ○ African safari?

What scares you? ______

Fave school subject? ______

Who's the worst of the fairy tale foes?

- ○ Wicked queen stepmother
- ○ Super mean stepsisters
- ○ Other ______

I LOVE TWISTER!

1. Name

2. Which have you taken a ride on? ○ Horse ○ Elephant ○ Camel ○ None!

3. Team (s) you like to root for? ______

4. Favorite pasta topping? ○ Meatballs ○ Cheese ○ Other______

5. ○ Pencil ○ Pen ○ Keyboard?

6. Own a pair of boots? ○ No ○ Yes, ______ pairs.

7. How 'bout a cowboy hat? ○ Yep ○ No way

8. Like peanut butter? ○ No ○ Yes, ______ is my favorite kind.

9. Think quiet people are ○ smart ○ shy ○ not interested?

10. Ideal summer vacation? ______

11. Play a mean game of ping pong? ○ Yep, I'm awesome. ○ I'm OK. ○ No!

12. Last time you played Twister? ______

13. ○ Zoo ○ Aquarium ○ Neither, I like animals in the wild.

14. Do you like Scrabble? ○ Yes ○ No

15. Singer/Band that appears the most on your playlists? ______

16. ZOMBIES ARE CHASING YOU. WHO DO YOU WANT WITH YOU? ______

17. Huge sale at the mall. Who would you want with you? ______

18. Tried raw oysters? ○ No ○ Yes Did you like? ○ No! Ick! ○ Yes

19. Three things for a perfect weekend? ______

20. Own anything with polka dots on it? ○ Of course ○ Nope

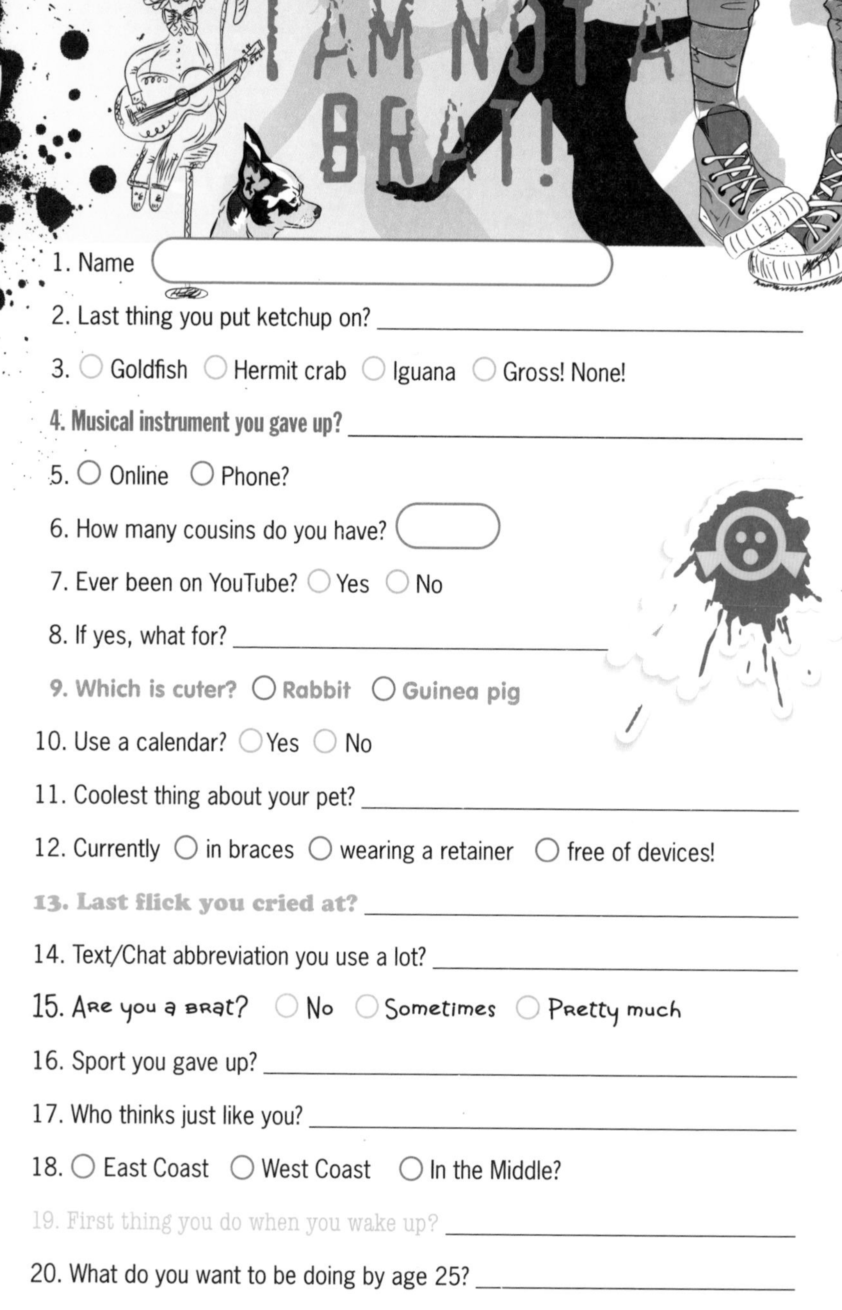

1. Name

2. Last thing you put ketchup on? ______

3. ○ Goldfish ○ Hermit crab ○ Iguana ○ Gross! None!

4. Musical instrument you gave up? ______

5. ○ Online ○ Phone?

6. How many cousins do you have?

7. Ever been on YouTube? ○ Yes ○ No

8. If yes, what for? ______

9. Which is cuter? ○ Rabbit ○ Guinea pig

10. Use a calendar? ○ Yes ○ No

11. Coolest thing about your pet? ______

12. Currently ○ in braces ○ wearing a retainer ○ free of devices!

13. Last flick you cried at? ______

14. Text/Chat abbreviation you use a lot? ______

15. Are you a brat? ○ No ○ Sometimes ○ Pretty much

16. Sport you gave up? ______

17. Who thinks just like you? ______

18. ○ East Coast ○ West Coast ○ In the Middle?

19. First thing you do when you wake up? ______

20. What do you want to be doing by age 25? ______

named that?

Do you like it?

Yes

No

Fave thing that comes in a wrapper?

Would you rather ...

Swim like a dolphin

Fly like an eagle?

Can you tie a good bow?

Yes

No

Where would you swim to?

Where would you fly to?

Do you interrrupt people?

Yes ☹

No ☺

Shake

Malt

What IS malt?

Fave flave?

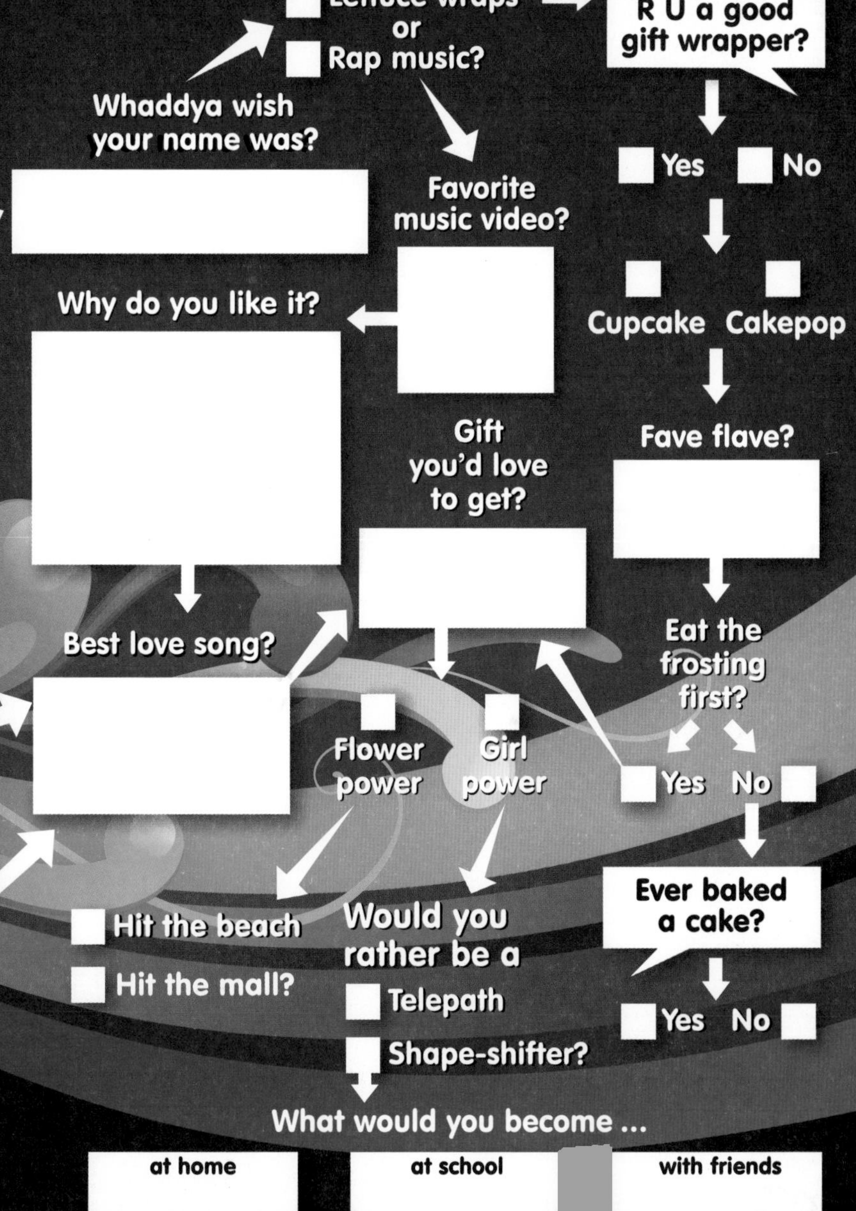

Lettuce wraps
or
Rap music?
R U a good gift wrapper?
Yes
No
Whaddya wish your name was?
Favorite music video?
Cupcake
Cakepop
Why do you like it?
Fave flave?
Gift you'd love to get?
Best love song?
Eat the frosting first?
Flower power
Girl power
Yes
No
Ever baked a cake?
Hit the beach
Hit the mall?
Would you rather be a
Telepath
Shape-shifter?
Yes
No
What would you become ...
at home
at school
with friends

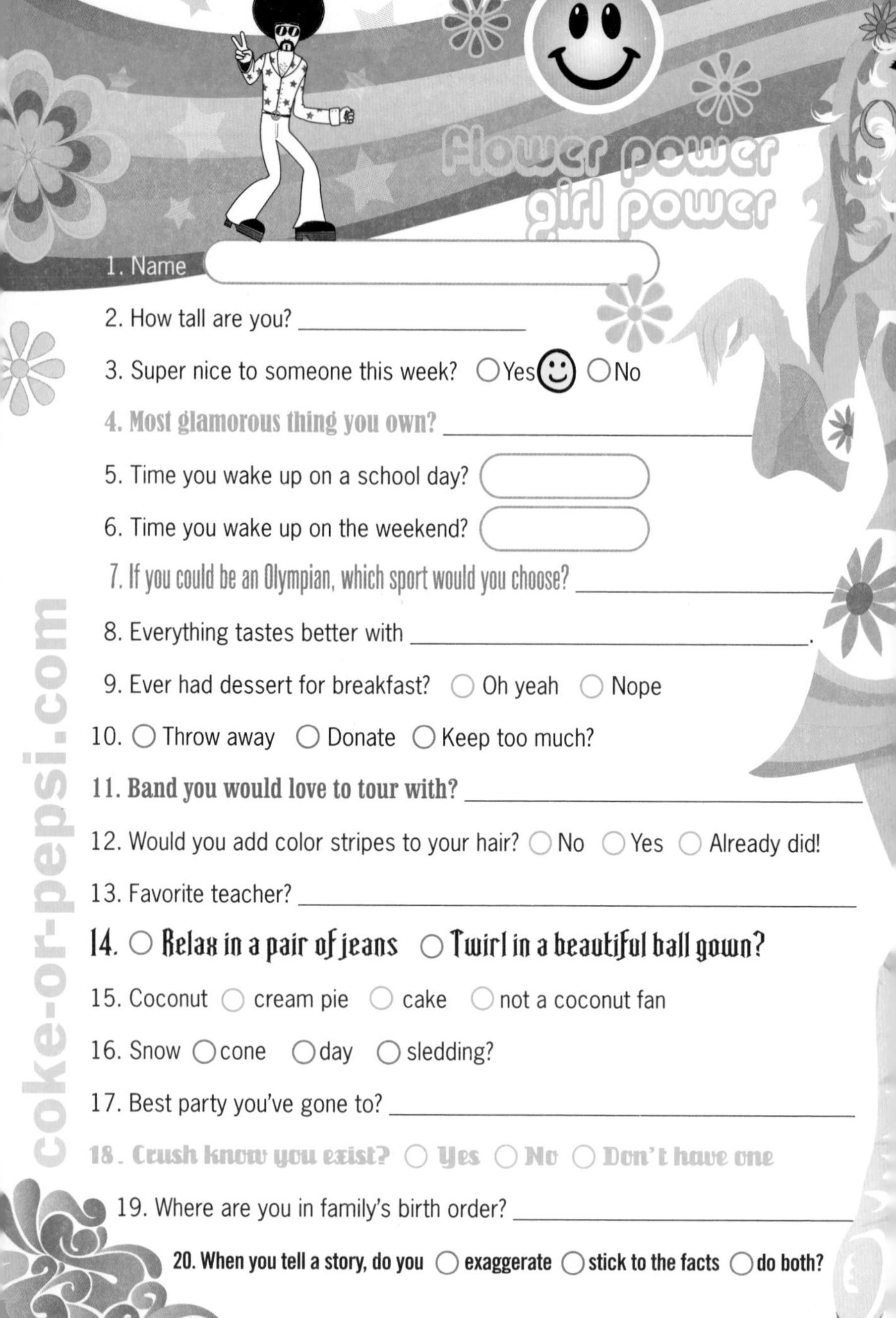

1. Name

2. How tall are you? ____________________

3. Super nice to someone this week? ○ Yes ○ No

4. Most glamorous thing you own? ____________________

5. Time you wake up on a school day?

6. Time you wake up on the weekend?

7. If you could be an Olympian, which sport would you choose? ____________________

8. Everything tastes better with ____________________.

9. Ever had dessert for breakfast? ○ Oh yeah ○ Nope

10. ○ Throw away ○ Donate ○ Keep too much?

11. Band you would love to tour with? ____________________

12. Would you add color stripes to your hair? ○ No ○ Yes ○ Already did!

13. Favorite teacher? ____________________

14. ○ Relax in a pair of jeans ○ Twirl in a beautiful ball gown?

15. Coconut ○ cream pie ○ cake ○ not a coconut fan

16. Snow ○ cone ○ day ○ sledding?

17. Best party you've gone to? ____________________

18. Crush know you exist? ○ Yes ○ No ○ Don't have one

19. Where are you in family's birth order? ____________________

20. When you tell a story, do you ○ exaggerate ○ stick to the facts ○ do both?

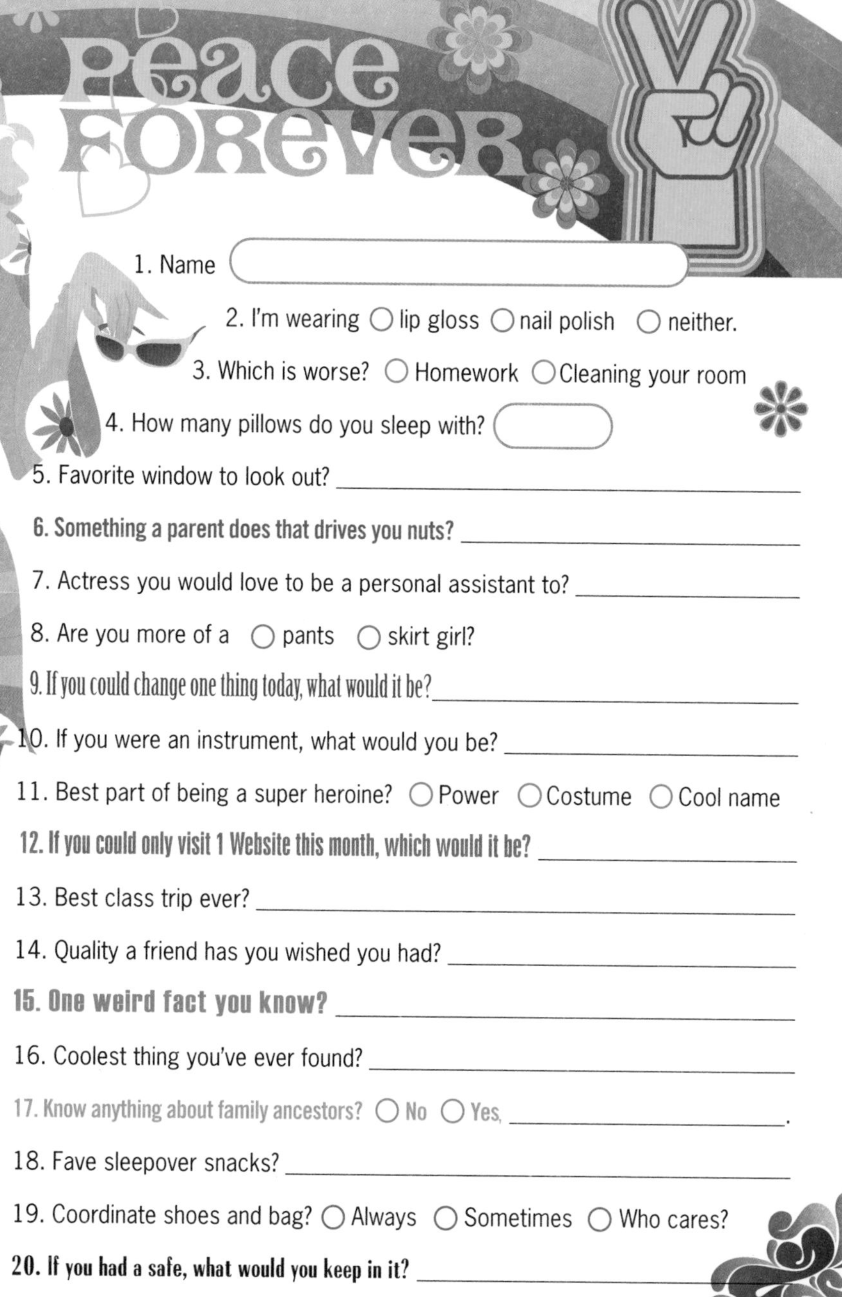

Peace Forever

1. Name

2. I'm wearing ◯ lip gloss ◯ nail polish ◯ neither.

3. Which is worse? ◯ Homework ◯ Cleaning your room

4. How many pillows do you sleep with?

5. Favorite window to look out? ______

6. Something a parent does that drives you nuts? ______

7. Actress you would love to be a personal assistant to? ______

8. Are you more of a ◯ pants ◯ skirt girl?

9. If you could change one thing today, what would it be? ______

10. If you were an instrument, what would you be? ______

11. Best part of being a super heroine? ◯ Power ◯ Costume ◯ Cool name

12. If you could only visit 1 Website this month, which would it be? ______

13. Best class trip ever? ______

14. Quality a friend has you wished you had? ______

15. One weird fact you know? ______

16. Coolest thing you've ever found? ______

17. Know anything about family ancestors? ◯ No ◯ Yes, ______.

18. Fave sleepover snacks? ______

19. Coordinate shoes and bag? ◯ Always ◯ Sometimes ◯ Who cares?

20. If you had a safe, what would you keep in it? ______

1. **a mermaid,** where in the world would you want to live? Why?

____

2. **President,** what kind of room would you add to the White House?

____

3. an exotic **animal keeper,** which animals would you want to care for?

____

4. **in charge** of naming the next kind of American spacecraft, what awesome name would you give it? _______________

5. **a dog,** which neighborhood dogs would you want to hang with? Why?

____

6. **a teacher,** what cool activity would you do with your class?

____

7. **in charge of your school** for a day, what would you change?

____

8. **going to live** on the moon for one year who would you take with you? Why? _______________

9. **able to stay** the same age for the rest of your life, which age would you pick? Why? _______________

10. able to have any **talent** you don't currently have, what would it be?

____

First thing that comes to mind when you see or hear these words?

(another word, sentence, or super short story)

1. Panda bear . . . .
2. Hysterical . . . .
3. Fireworks . . . .
4. T-shirt . . . .
5. Marshmallow . . . .
6. Celery sticks . . . .
7. Raisins . . . .
8. Poodle . . . .
9. Sunglasses . . . .
10. Chucks . . . .
11. Stick people . . . .
12. Physical Education . . . .
13. Mountain . . . .
14. Scooter . . . .
15. Pyramid . . . .
16. Diamonds . . . .
17. Hot peppers . . . .
18. Ringtone . . . .
19. Nail polish . . . .
20. Alligator . . . .

Name

1. Name

2. ○ Cinnamon ○ Fruity ○ Minty gum?

3. What do you love about yourself? ______

4. Where were you last time you used mustard? ______

5. The last paper I wrote for a class was about ______

______.

6. I could never eat ______ again and be OK.

7. TV show you most belong on? ______

8. WOULD YOU RATHER BE THE ○ STAR ON A LOSING TEAM ○ WORST ON A STAR TEAM?

9. Ever carved anything in a tree? ○ Yes ○ No

10. ○ Swim with the dolphins ○ Pet a manatee?

11. Would you rather be a ○ giant ○ pixie?

12. ○ Fuzzy socks ○ Warm slippers?

13. Hot chocolate ○ with ○ without marshmallows?

14. Good at sneaking up on people? ○ Not really ○ Kind of ○ Absolutely!

15. Scariest thing you've done on purpose? ______

16. New pair of ○ jeans ○ shoes?

17. If I could ______, I would be thrilled.

18. Age you turned on fave birthday?

19. Something you would love to see? ______

20. Which is worse? ○ Really sad ○ Out-of-control mad

Potato chips
French fries?
coke
OR
pepsi?
classic
Fashionable
Casual?
Sunset
Sunrise?
Brownies
Chocolate chip cookies?
Best holiday?
Fave actor?
Fave actress?
One word to describe you?
Big Mac
Whopper?
Gold
Silver?
coke-or-pepsi.com

forever

1. Name

2. ◯ Skinny jeans ◯ Jeggings ◯ Neither?

3. Happiest color? ______________________

4. What were you doing in the last photo taken of you? ______________________

5. Where were you? ______________________

6. Know how to cook? ◯ **No** ◯ **A little** ◯ **Yes**

7. If yes to #6, what's your specialty? ______________________

8. Are you usually ◯ cold ◯ hot?

9. Famous person you admire most? ______________________

10. DO HORROR MOVIES FRIGHTEN YOU? ◯ NOT REALLY ◯ YES, NIGHTMARES!

11. Fave outfit to relax in? ______________________

12. Ever shoot a spitball? ◯ Yes ◯ Gross, no!

13. Favorite thing that comes in your mail? ______________________.

14. Sprinkles ◯ always make me happy ◯ are kinda overrated.

15. Any phobias or fears? ◯ Nope ◯ Yes, I'm afraid of ______________________.

16. ◯ Drama queen ◯ Cool, calm, and collected?

17. What do you crave? ______________________

18. Drink after other people? ◯ Yeah ◯ Sometimes ◯ Never! Germs!

19. Ever encountered a bat? ◯ Yes ◯ No

20. What do you hear right now? ______________________

1. Name ______

2. Afraid to cross bridges? ◯ Yes ◯ No

3. Can you wiggle your ears without using your hands? ◯ No ◯ Yes

4. Do you ◯ give in ◯ get your way?

5. LAST THING YOU SOLD FOR YOUR SCHOOL? ______

6. Go to the library? ◯ No ◯ Yes

7. Longest word you know? ______

8. Can you hang a spoon from your nose? ◯ Yes ◯ No ◯ Huh?

9. Best food with a glass of milk? ______

10. Gold ◯ fish ◯ bracelet?

11. Any strange talent? ◯ No ◯ Yes, I ______.

12. Spend the night in a haunted house? ◯ NO! ◯ Sure, I don't believe.

13. It's scary how much I like ______.

14. Give good manicures? ◯ Yes ◯ No

15. Favorite reality show? ______

16. Scrambled eggs are ◯ yummy ◯ frightening.

17. Worst thing about your brother(s)/sister(s)? ______

18. Best thing about your brother(s)/sister(s)? ______

19. LOVE A GOOD MYSTERY? ◯ YES! ◯ NAH

20. Think you're creative? ◯ Yes ◯ A little ◯ Not really

1. swim with a huge, harmless whale in the ocean, would you? ○Yes ○No, but I would swim with ______.

2. slow down time, which event would you slow down? ______

3. add sisters or brothers to your family, which genders and ages would you choose? ______

4. have absolutely anything for dinner tonight, what would you pick? ______

5. do one fun thing with an alien visiting our planet, what would it be? ______

6. become any object for just one day, what would you be? Why? ______

7. be an exchange student for one year anywhere in the world, which country would you visit? ______

8. be great friends with someone from the past, who would you choose? Why? ______

9. do absolutely anything for just one year, what would you do? ______

10. change your last name, without hurting your parents' feelings, would you?
○ No ○ Yes, I would change it to ______.

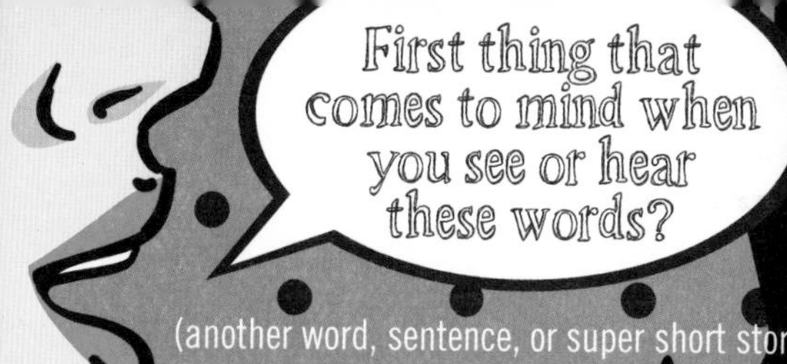

(another word, sentence, or super short story)

Name

1. Corn on the cob . . . .
2. Dark alley . . . .
3. Roller coaster . . . .
4. Pigs in blankets . . . .
5. Hamster . . . .
6. Pink . . . .
7. Glow-in-the-dark . . . .
8. The letter U . . . .
9. Hello Kitty . . . .
10. Face painting . . . .
11. Super star . . . .
12. Bell . . . .
13. Sleeping bag . . . .
14. Hollywood . . . .
15. Rock . . . .
16. Piano . . . .
17. Magazine . . . .
18. Watermelon . . . .
19. Bubbles . . . .
20. Subway . . . .

classic

- Waffle cone
- Sugar cone
- Cup?

- Ice cubes
- Crushed ice?

- TV
- Book?

- Beach
- Mountains?

- Go with the flow
- Stick to a routine?

- Ice cream
- Fro-yo?

Favorite relative?

Best amusement park ride?

Favorite game?

Best book?

last things i painted were my nails

1. Name

2. Best thing in a spray can? ◯ **Whipped Cream** ◯ **Cheese Whiz** ◯ **Paint**

3. Ever sprayed whipped cream directly in your mouth? ◯ Yes ◯ No

4. Last thing you painted? ______

5. Last thing you had stuck in your hair? ______

6. ◯ Donuts ◯ Donut holes

7. Worse T-shirt color? ◯ **Orange** ◯ **Yellow** ◯ **Green**

8. What are you a beginner at? ______

9. What are you an expert at? ______

10. Favorite dip? ______

11. Favorite thing to dip? ______

12. Scarves? ◯ Luv 'em ◯ Hate 'em, so restricting!

13. I heart ______.

14. ______ is epic.

15. Friend with the coolest family? ______

16. ◯ Red velvet cheesecake brownie ◯ S'more-stuffed chocolate chip cookie?

17. Fave flave for lipgloss? ______

18. Favorite emoticon? ______

19. ◯ Abracadabra ◯ Bipiddi-boppidi-boo ◯ Expelliarmus?

20. ◯ Lemonade ◯ Pink Lemonade?

PRIVATE

I like movies that make me cry

1. Name

2. Last animated movie you saw? ____________

3. Movies ○ with happy endings ○ that leave you thinking?

4. Sleepovers? ○ Fun! ○ Ugh.

5. ○ French Bulldog ○ Irish Setter ○ Alaskan Husky?

6. **Movies** ○ **at the theater** ○ **at home?**

7. Are you a ○ share-your-umbrella ○ every-girl-for-herself kinda girl?

8. ○ Polo ○ Graphic Tee?

9. Love to see a ○ volcano erupt ○ total eclipse of the sun?

10. What does your hair do on rainy days? ____________

11. ○ **Write a great novel** ○ **Travel around the world?**

12. ○ Hike through the woods ○ Stroll through the city?

13. Ever danced the hula? ○ Yes ○ No

14. **Very first song you remember liking?** ____________

15. Maple syrup on ○ waffles ○ French toast?

16. Ever fallen backwards in a chair? ○ Yes ○ No

17. **Wear shoes in the house?** ○ **Yes** ○ **Sometimes** ○ **Never**

18. If you get married, will you ○ keep ○ ditch ○ combine your last name(s)?

19. ○ Pack light ○ Certified overpacker?

20. FAVE SONG TO SING ON ROCK BAND OR GUITAR HERO? ____________

I'll never get rid of my chucks

1. Name

2. On anyone's bad side right now? ○ Yes ○ No

3. WORN-OUT ITEM YOU CAN'T PART WITH? ____________

4. ○ Italian ice ○ French vanilla ice cream ○ German chocolate cake?

5. Most unusual animal you've ever fed? ____________

6. When things get hard, do you usually ○ give up ○ keep trying?

7. SCHOOL UNIFORMS? ○ FOR IT ○ AGAINST?

8. ○ Sweater ○ Hoodie?

9. One thing you'd like to learn to do well? ____________

10. Pigs are ○ so cute ○ muddy, stinky, and gross.

11. Wear glitter? ○ Yes, love the sparkle! ○ Nah, too gaudy.

12. Glow sticks? ○ Still fun ○ Ho hum

13. Last thing you do before you turn off the lights? ____________

14. Love ○ notes ○ letter ○ potion?

15. ○ Brownie ○ Girl Scout ○ Other ____________ ○ None?

16. Favorite Girl Scout cookie? ____________

17. Lucky charm or something lucky you wear? ○ No ○ Yes, ____________.

18. Ever run a lemonade stand? ○ Yes ○ No

19. Kind of business you'd like to start someday? ____________

20. **I would love to be president of ____________.**

Twofers

Name

1. Fave sweet and salty combo?____________________

2. Reasons for being late?____________________

3. Things you always have with you?____________________

4. Fave furry animals?____________________

5. Habits you have?____________________

6. Stuff outside your bedroom window?____________________

7. Places you love?____________________

8. Things you've climbed?____________________

9. Words you really love?____________________

10. Qualities you like in a friend?____________________

11. Things that make you mad?____________________

12. Fave animals that swim in the sea?____________________

13. Green things you'll eat?____________________

14. Black and white things you like?____________________

15. Beverages you drink almost every day?____________________

16. Things you love that fit in your hand?____________________

17. Friends you talk to almost every day?____________________

18. Colors you like to paint your toenails?____________________

19. Stuff you've won?____________________

20. Things you've lost?____________________

1 question.
2 answers.

forever.

are so cute!

are awesome words!

are my favorites.

are missing.

1. Name

2. Leopard prints are so ○ chic ○ tacky?

3. ○ **Seven dwarves** ○ **One fairy godmother?**

4. How many tiaras do you own?

5. Mannequins give you the creeps? ○ No ○ Yes

6. Ever been in a corn maze? ○ Yes ○ No ○ Not sure, what is that?

7. **Last school project you did?** ______________________________

8. British accents sound ○ so cool ○ smart ○ kinda snobby?

9. ○ Pair of glass slippers ○ Pumpkin that turns into a carriage?

10. **Magic ○ potion ○ wand ○ markers?**

11. ○ Sand between your toes ○ Out too deep to touch bottom?

12. Bowling? ○ Ridiculous ○ Fun ○ Ridiculously fun!

13. **What do you talk about more than anything?** ______________________________

14. Would you rather be a ○ princess ○ princess' sister?

15. Skinny jeans with ○ flats ○ flip-flops ○ sneakers?

16. Today are you ○ fairest of them all ○ "sleepy" beauty?

17. Three words to describe your life? ______________________________

18. Favorite song to sing with friends? ______________________________

19. How 'bout to dance to with friends? ______________________________

20. **I wish I were a(n) ○ English ○ history ○ math ○ science whiz!**

Who's the worst of the fairy tale foes?

- ○ Wicked queen step-mother
- ○ Super mean step-sisters
- ○ Other

____

____

coke OR pepsi?

classic

- ● Coke ● Pepsi?
- ● Hot dog ● Hamburger?
- ● Milk ● Dark chocolate?
- ● Butterflies ● Dragonflies?
- ● Small talk
  ● Deep conversation?
- ● Sneakers ● Flip-flops?

Best movie ever? _______________

____

Worst movie ever? _______________

____

Favorite number? Why? _______________

____

- ● Reality show ● Sitcom?
- ● Bicycle through Europe
  ● African safari?

What scares you? _______________

____

Fave school subject? _______________

____

I LOVE TWISTER!

1. Name

2. Which have you taken a ride on? ○ **Horse** ○ **Elephant** ○ **Camel** ○ **None!**

3. Team(s) you like to root for? ______________________

4. Favorite pasta topping? ○ Meatballs ○ Cheese ○ Other______________

5. ○ Pencil ○ Pen ○ Keyboard?

6. Own a pair of boots? ○ **No** ○ **Yes,** ______ **pairs.**

7. How 'bout a cowboy hat? ○ Yep ○ No way

8. Like peanut butter? ○ No ○ Yes, ______________ is my favorite kind.

9. Think quiet people are ○ smart ○ shy ○ not interested?

10. Ideal summer vacation? ______________________

11. Play a mean game of ping pong? ○ Yep, I'm awesome. ○ I'm OK. ○ No!

12. Last time you played Twister? ______________________

13. ○ Zoo ○ Aquarium ○ Neither, I like animals in the wild.

14. Do you like Scrabble? ○ Yes ○ No

15. Singer/Band that appears the most on your playlists? ______________

16. ZOMBIES ARE CHASING YOU. WHO DO YOU WANT WITH YOU? ______________

17. Huge sale at the mall. Who would you want with you? ______________

18. Tried raw oysters? ○ No ○ Yes Did you like? ○ No! Ick! ○ Yes

19. Three things for a perfect weekend? ______________________

20. Own anything with polka dots on it? ○ Of course ○ Nope

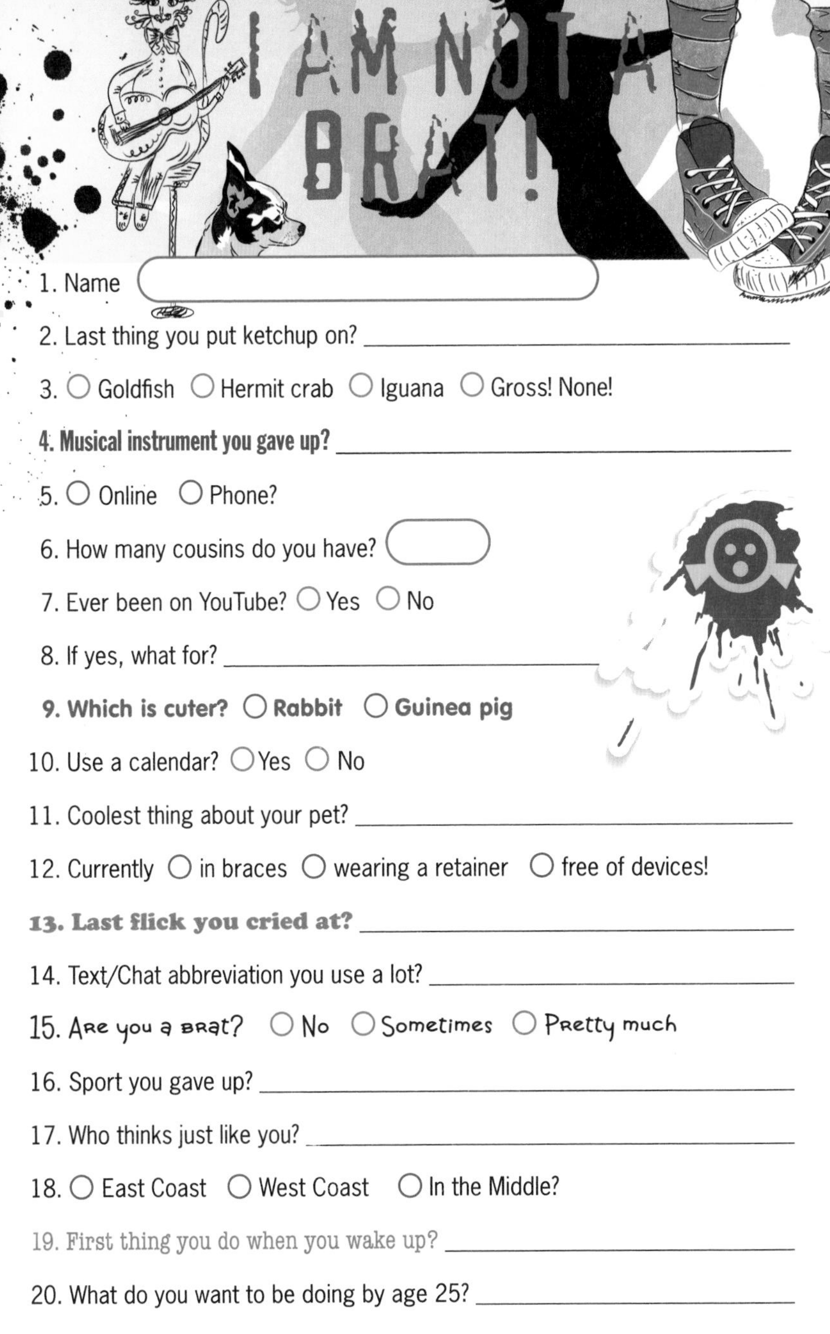

1. Name

2. Last thing you put ketchup on? ______

3. ○ Goldfish ○ Hermit crab ○ Iguana ○ Gross! None!

4. Musical instrument you gave up? ______

5. ○ Online ○ Phone?

6. How many cousins do you have?

7. Ever been on YouTube? ○ Yes ○ No

8. If yes, what for? ______

9. Which is cuter? ○ Rabbit ○ Guinea pig

10. Use a calendar? ○ Yes ○ No

11. Coolest thing about your pet? ______

12. Currently ○ in braces ○ wearing a retainer ○ free of devices!

13. Last flick you cried at? ______

14. Text/Chat abbreviation you use a lot? ______

15. Are you a brat? ○ No ○ Sometimes ○ Pretty much

16. Sport you gave up? ______

17. Who thinks just like you? ______

18. ○ East Coast ○ West Coast ○ In the Middle?

19. First thing you do when you wake up? ______

20. What do you want to be doing by age 25? ______

named that?

Fave thing that comes in a wrapper?

Can you tie a good bow?

Yes

No

Do you interrrupt people?

Yes ☹

No ☺

Shake

Malt

Fave flave?

Do you like it?

Yes

No

Would you rather ...

Swim like a dolphin

Fly like an eagle?

Where would you swim to?

Where would you fly to?

What IS malt?

coke-or-pepsi.com

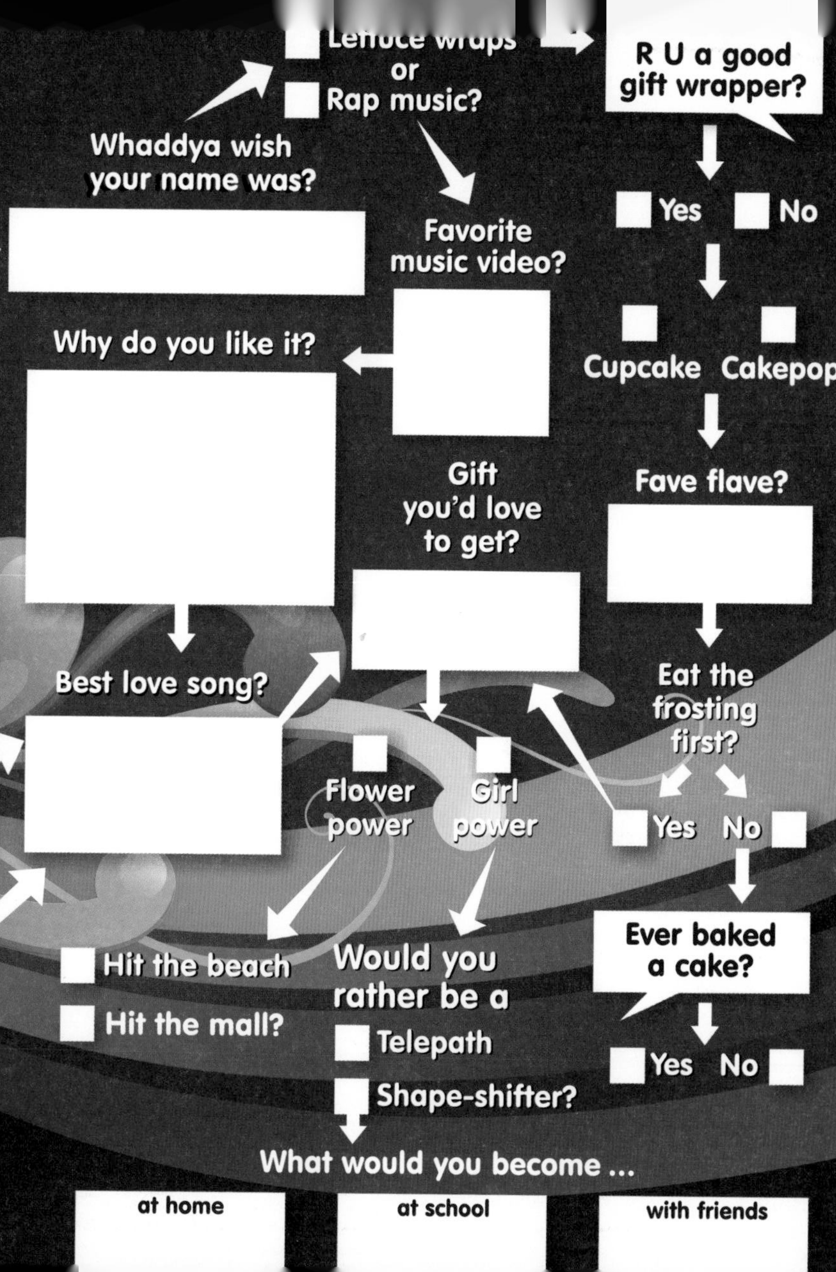

Lettuce wraps
or
Rap music?
R U a good gift wrapper?
Whaddya wish your name was?
Yes
No
Favorite music video?
Cupcake
Cakepop
Why do you like it?
Gift you'd love to get?
Fave flave?
Best love song?
Eat the frosting first?
Flower power
Girl power
Yes
No
Ever baked a cake?
Hit the beach
Hit the mall?
Would you rather be a
Telepath
Shape-shifter?
Yes
No
What would you become ...
at home
at school
with friends

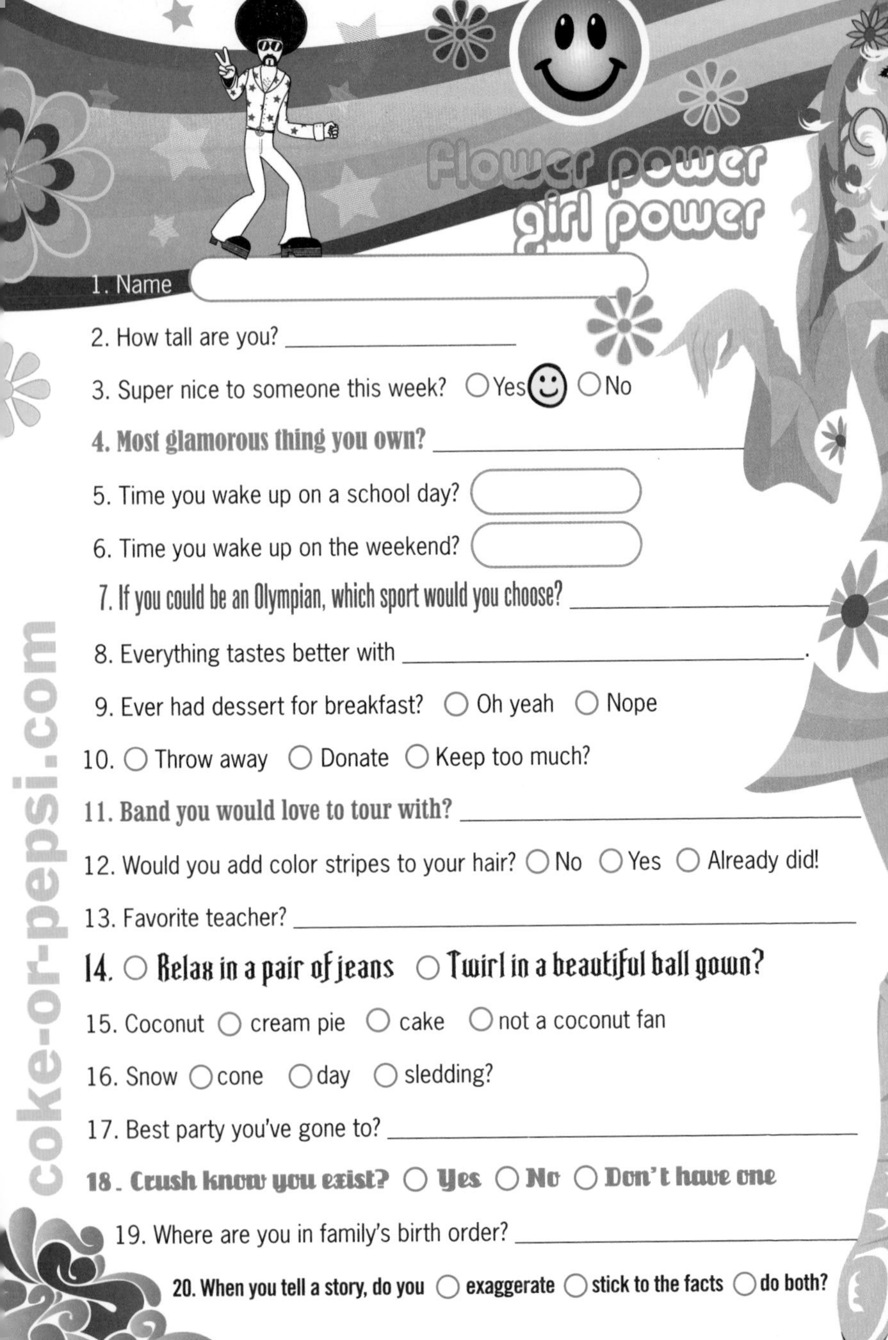

1. Name

2. How tall are you? ____________

3. Super nice to someone this week? ◯ Yes ◯ No

4. **Most glamorous thing you own?** ____________

5. Time you wake up on a school day?

6. Time you wake up on the weekend?

7. If you could be an Olympian, which sport would you choose? ____________

8. Everything tastes better with ____________.

9. Ever had dessert for breakfast? ◯ Oh yeah ◯ Nope

10. ◯ Throw away ◯ Donate ◯ Keep too much?

11. **Band you would love to tour with?** ____________

12. Would you add color stripes to your hair? ◯ No ◯ Yes ◯ Already did!

13. Favorite teacher? ____________

14. ◯ Relax in a pair of jeans ◯ Twirl in a beautiful ball gown?

15. Coconut ◯ cream pie ◯ cake ◯ not a coconut fan

16. Snow ◯ cone ◯ day ◯ sledding?

17. Best party you've gone to? ____________

18. **Crush know you exist? ◯ Yes ◯ No ◯ Don't have one**

19. Where are you in family's birth order? ____________

20. **When you tell a story, do you ◯ exaggerate ◯ stick to the facts ◯ do both?**

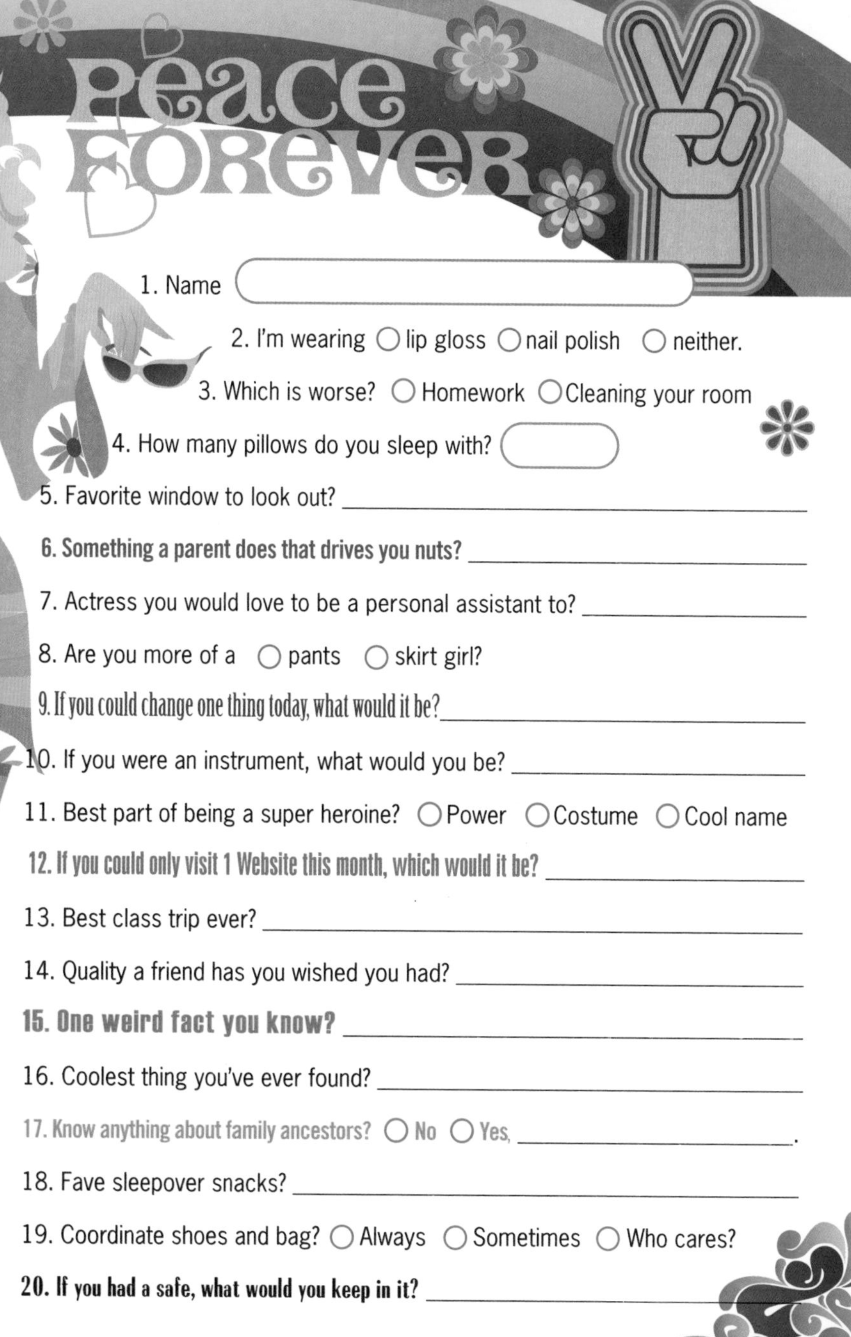

Peace Forever

1. Name

2. I'm wearing ◯ lip gloss ◯ nail polish ◯ neither.

3. Which is worse? ◯ Homework ◯ Cleaning your room

4. How many pillows do you sleep with?

5. Favorite window to look out? ______

6. Something a parent does that drives you nuts? ______

7. Actress you would love to be a personal assistant to? ______

8. Are you more of a ◯ pants ◯ skirt girl?

9. If you could change one thing today, what would it be? ______

10. If you were an instrument, what would you be? ______

11. Best part of being a super heroine? ◯ Power ◯ Costume ◯ Cool name

12. If you could only visit 1 Website this month, which would it be? ______

13. Best class trip ever? ______

14. Quality a friend has you wished you had? ______

15. One weird fact you know? ______

16. Coolest thing you've ever found? ______

17. Know anything about family ancestors? ◯ No ◯ Yes, ______.

18. Fave sleepover snacks? ______

19. Coordinate shoes and bag? ◯ Always ◯ Sometimes ◯ Who cares?

20. If you had a safe, what would you keep in it? ______

1. **a mermaid,** where in the world would you want to live? Why?

____

2. **President,** what kind of room would you add to the White House?

____

3. an exotic **animal keeper,** which animals would you want to care for?

____

4. **in charge** of naming the next kind of American spacecraft, what awesome name would you give it? _______________

5. **a dog,** which neighborhood dogs would you want to hang with? Why?

____

6. **a teacher,** what cool activity would you do with your class?

____

7. **in charge of your school** for a day, what would you change?

____

8. **going to live** on the moon for one year who would you take with you? Why? _______________

9. **able to stay** the same age for the rest of your life, which age would you pick? Why? _______________

10. able to have any **talent** you don't currently have, what would it be?

____

First thing that comes to mind when you see or hear these words?

(another word, sentence, or super short story)

1. Panda bear . . . .
2. Hysterical . . . .
3. Fireworks . . . .
4. T-shirt . . . .
5. Marshmallow . . . .
6. Celery sticks . . . .
7. Raisins . . . .
8. Poodle . . . .
9. Sunglasses . . . .
10. Chucks . . . .
11. Stick people . . . .
12. Physical Education . . . .
13. Mountain . . . .
14. Scooter . . . .
15. Pyramid . . . .
16. Diamonds . . . .
17. Hot peppers . . . .
18. Ringtone . . . .
19. Nail polish . . . .
20. Alligator . . . .

Name

1. Name

2. ○ Cinnamon ○ Fruity ○ Minty gum?

3. What do you love about yourself? ______________________

4. Where were you last time you used mustard? ______________________

5. The last paper I wrote for a class was about ______________________

____.

6. I could never eat ______________________ again and be OK.

7. TV show you most belong on? ______________________

8. WOULD YOU RATHER BE THE ○ STAR ON A LOSING TEAM ○ WORST ON A STAR TEAM?

9. Ever carved anything in a tree? ○ Yes ○ No

10. ○ Swim with the dolphins ○ Pet a manatee?

11. Would you rather be a ○ giant ○ pixie?

12. ○ Fuzzy socks ○ Warm slippers?

13. Hot chocolate ○ with ○ without marshmallows?

14. Good at sneaking up on people? ○ Not really ○ Kind of ○ Absolutely!

15. Scariest thing you've done on purpose? ______________________

16. New pair of ○ jeans ○ shoes?

17. If I could ______________________, I would be thrilled.

18. Age you turned on fave birthday?

19. Something you would love to see? ______________________

20. Which is worse? ○ Really sad ○ Out-of-control mad

Potato chips
French fries?
Fashionable
Casual?
Sunset
Sunrise?
Brownies
Chocolate chip cookies?
coke
OR
pepsi?
classic
Best holiday?
Fave actor?
Fave actress?
One word to describe you?
Big Mac
Whopper?
Gold
Silver?
coke-or-pepsi.com

forever

1. Name ____________________

2. ○ Skinny jeans ○ Jeggings ○ Neither?

3. *Happiest color?* ____________________

4. What were you doing in the last photo taken of you? ____________________

5. Where were you? ____________________

6. Know how to cook? ○ **No** ○ **A little** ○ **Yes**

7. If yes to #6, what's your specialty? ____________________

8. Are you usually ○ cold ○ hot?

9. Famous person you admire most? ____________________

10. DO HORROR MOVIES FRIGHTEN YOU? ○ **NOT REALLY** ○ **YES, NIGHTMARES!**

11. Fave outfit to relax in? ____________________

12. Ever shoot a spitball? ○ Yes ○ Gross, no!

13. Favorite thing that comes in your mail? ____________________.

14. Sprinkles ○ always make me happy ○ are kinda overrated.

15. Any phobias or fears? ○ Nope ○ Yes, I'm afraid of ____________________.

16. ○ Drama queen ○ Cool, calm, and collected?

17. What do you crave? ____________________

18. Drink after other people? ○ Yeah ○ Sometimes ○ Never! Germs!

19. Ever encountered a bat? ○ Yes ○ No

20. What do you hear right now? ____________________

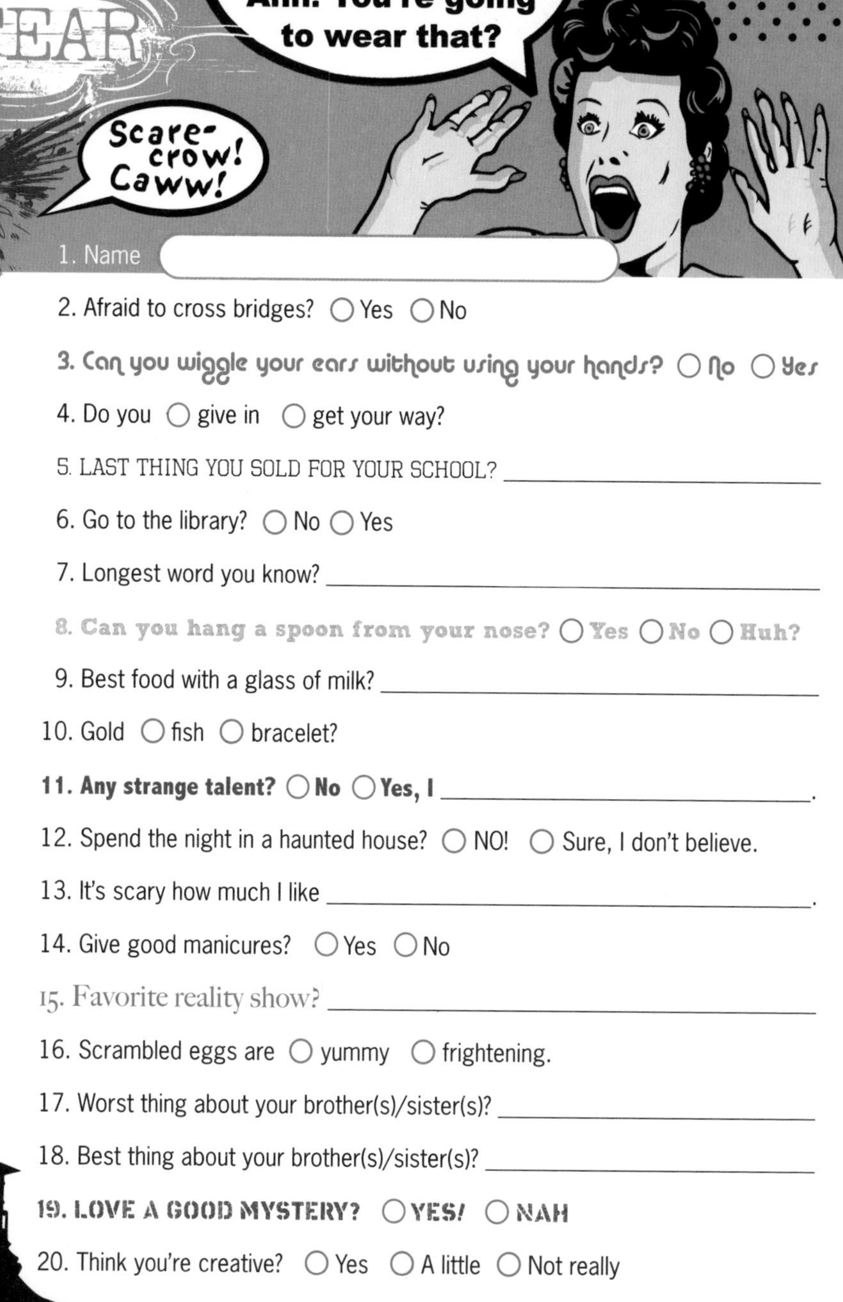

1. Name

2. Afraid to cross bridges? ○ Yes ○ No

3. Can you wiggle your ears without using your hands? ○ No ○ Yes

4. Do you ○ give in ○ get your way?

5. LAST THING YOU SOLD FOR YOUR SCHOOL? ______

6. Go to the library? ○ No ○ Yes

7. Longest word you know? ______

8. Can you hang a spoon from your nose? ○ Yes ○ No ○ Huh?

9. Best food with a glass of milk? ______

10. Gold ○ fish ○ bracelet?

11. Any strange talent? ○ No ○ Yes, I ______.

12. Spend the night in a haunted house? ○ NO! ○ Sure, I don't believe.

13. It's scary how much I like ______.

14. Give good manicures? ○ Yes ○ No

15. Favorite reality show? ______

16. Scrambled eggs are ○ yummy ○ frightening.

17. Worst thing about your brother(s)/sister(s)? ______

18. Best thing about your brother(s)/sister(s)? ______

19. LOVE A GOOD MYSTERY? ○ YES! ○ NAH

20. Think you're creative? ○ Yes ○ A little ○ Not really

Name

1. swim with a huge, harmless whale in the ocean, would you? ○Yes ○No, but I would swim with ______.
2. slow down time, which event would you slow down? ______
3. add sisters or brothers to your family, which genders and ages would you choose? ______
4. have absolutely anything for dinner tonight, what would you pick? ______
5. do one fun thing with an alien visiting our planet, what would it be? ______
6. become any object for just one day, what would you be? Why? ______
7. be an exchange student for one year anywhere in the world, which country would you visit? ______
8. be great friends with someone from the past, who would you choose? Why? ______
9. do absolutely anything for just one year, what would you do? ______
10. change your last name, without hurting your parents' feelings, would you?

    ○ No ○ Yes, I would change it to ______.

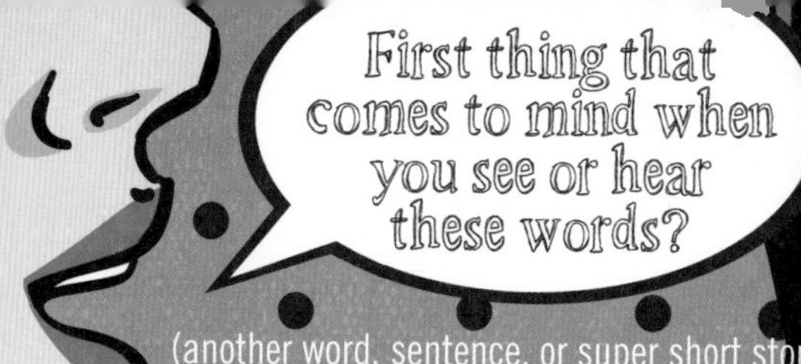

(another word, sentence, or super short story)

Name

1. Corn on the cob . . . .
2. Dark alley . . . .
3. Roller coaster . . . .
4. Pigs in blankets . . . .
5. Hamster . . . .
6. Pink . . . .
7. Glow-in-the-dark . . . .
8. The letter U . . . .
9. Hello Kitty . . . .
10. Face painting . . . .
11. Super star . . . .
12. Bell . . . .
13. Sleeping bag . . . .
14. Hollywood . . . .
15. Rock . . . .
16. Piano . . . .
17. Magazine . . . .
18. Watermelon . . . .
19. Bubbles . . . .
20. Subway . . . .

coke OR pepsi?

classic

- ◯ Waffle cone
- ◯ Sugar cone
- ◯ Cup?

- ◯ Ice cubes
- ◯ Crushed ice?

- ◯ TV
- ◯ Book?

- ◯ Beach
- ◯ Mountains?

- ◯ Go with the flow
- ◯ Stick to a routine?

- ◯ Ice cream
- ◯ Fro-yo?

Favorite relative?

Best amusement park ride?

Favorite game?

Best book?

coke-or-pepsi.com

last things i painted were my nails

1. Name ____________________

2. Best thing in a spray can? ○ Whipped Cream ○ Cheese Whiz ○ Paint

3. Ever sprayed whipped cream directly in your mouth? ○ Yes ○ No

4. Last thing you painted? ____________________

5. Last thing you had stuck in your hair? ____________________

6. ○ Donuts ○ Donut holes

7. **Worse T-shirt color?** ○ Orange ○ Yellow ○ Green

8. What are you a beginner at? ____________________

9. What are you an expert at? ____________________

10. **Favorite dip?** ____________________

11. Favorite thing to dip? ____________________

12. Scarves? ○ Luv 'em ○ Hate 'em, so restricting!

13. I heart ____________________.

14. ____________________ is epic.

15. Friend with the coolest family? ____________________

16. ○ Red velvet cheesecake brownie ○ S'more-stuffed chocolate chip cookie?

17. Fave flave for lipgloss? ____________________

18. Favorite emoticon? ____________________

19. ○ Abracadabra ○ Bipiddi-boppidi-boo ○ Expelliarmus?

20. ○ Lemonade ○ Pink Lemonade?

PRIVATE

I like movies that make me cry

1. Name ______

2. Last animated movie you saw? ______

3. Movies ○ with happy endings ○ that leave you thinking?

4. Sleepovers? ○ Fun! ○ Ugh.

5. ○ French Bulldog ○ Irish Setter ○ Alaskan Husky?

6. **Movies ○ at the theater ○ at home?**

7. Are you a ○ share-your-umbrella ○ every-girl-for-herself kinda girl?

8. ○ Polo ○ Graphic Tee?

9. Love to see a ○ volcano erupt ○ total eclipse of the sun?

10. What does your hair do on rainy days? ______

11. **○ Write a great novel ○ Travel around the world?**

12. ○ Hike through the woods ○ Stroll through the city?

13. Ever danced the hula? ○ Yes ○ No

14. **Very first song you remember liking?** ______

15. Maple syrup on ○ waffles ○ French toast?

16. Ever fallen backwards in a chair? ○ Yes ○ No

17. **Wear shoes in the house? ○ Yes ○ Sometimes ○ Never**

18. If you get married, will you ○ keep ○ ditch ○ combine your last name(s)?

19. ○ Pack light ○ Certified overpacker?

20. FAVE SONG TO SING ON ROCK BAND OR GUITAR HERO? ______

I'll never get rid of my chucks

1. Name ______

2. On anyone's bad side right now? ○ Yes ○ No

3. WORN-OUT ITEM YOU CAN'T PART WITH? ______

4. ○ Italian ice ○ French vanilla ice cream ○ German chocolate cake?

5. Most unusual animal you've ever fed? ______

6. When things get hard, do you usually ○ give up ○ keep trying?

7. SCHOOL UNIFORMS? ○ FOR IT ○ AGAINST?

8. ○ Sweater ○ Hoodie?

9. One thing you'd like to learn to do well? ______

10. Pigs are ○ so cute ○ muddy, stinky, and gross.

11. Wear glitter? ○ Yes, love the sparkle! ○ Nah, too gaudy.

12. Glow sticks? ○ Still fun ○ Ho hum

13. Last thing you do before you turn off the lights? ______

14. Love ○ notes ○ letter ○ potion?

15. ○ Brownie ○ Girl Scout ○ Other ______ ○ None?

16. Favorite Girl Scout cookie? ______

17. Lucky charm or something lucky you wear? ○ No ○ Yes, ______.

18. Ever run a lemonade stand? ○ Yes ○ No

19. Kind of business you'd like to start someday? ______

20. **I would love to be president of ______.**

Twofers

Name

1. Fave sweet and salty combo? ______
2. Reasons for being late? ______
3. Things you always have with you? ______
4. Fave furry animals? ______
5. Habits you have? ______
6. Stuff outside your bedroom window? ______
7. Places you love? ______
8. Things you've climbed? ______
9. Words you really love? ______
10. Qualities you like in a friend? ______
11. Things that make you mad? ______
12. Fave animals that swim in the sea? ______
13. Green things you'll eat? ______
14. Black and white things you like? ______
15. Beverages you drink almost every day? ______
16. Things you love that fit in your hand? ______
17. Friends you talk to almost every day? ______
18. Colors you like to paint your toenails? ______
19. Stuff you've won? ______
20. Things you've lost? ______

1 question. 2 answers.

______________________________ forever.

______________________________ are so cute!

______________________________ are awesome words!

______________________________ are my favorites.

______________________________ are missing.

1. Name

2. Leopard prints are so ○ chic ○ tacky?

3. ○ Seven dwarves ○ One fairy godmother?

4. How many tiaras do you own?

5. Mannequins give you the creeps? ○ No ○ Yes

6. Ever been in a corn maze? ○ Yes ○ No ○ Not sure, what is that?

7. Last school project you did? ______________________

8. British accents sound ○ so cool ○ smart ○ kinda snobby?

9. ○ Pair of glass slippers ○ Pumpkin that turns into a carriage?

10. Magic ○ potion ○ wand ○ markers?

11. ○ Sand between your toes ○ Out too deep to touch bottom?

12. Bowling? ○ Ridiculous ○ Fun ○ Ridiculously fun!

13. What do you talk about more than anything? ______________________

14. Would you rather be a ○ princess ○ princess' sister?

15. Skinny jeans with ○ flats ○ flip-flops ○ sneakers?

16. Today are you ○ fairest of them all ○ "sleepy" beauty?

17. Three words to describe your life? ______________________

18. Favorite song to sing with friends? ______________________

19. How 'bout to dance to with friends? ______________________

20. I wish I were a(n) ○ English ○ history ○ math ○ science whiz!

Who's the worst of the fairy tale foes?

- ○ Wicked queen step-mother
- ○ Super mean step-sisters
- ○ Other ______________

coke OR pepsi?

classic

- ○ Coke ○ Pepsi?
- ○ Hot dog ○ Hamburger?
- ○ Milk ○ Dark chocolate?
- ○ Butterflies ○ Dragonflies?
- ○ Small talk
- ○ Deep conversation?
- ○ Sneakers ○ Flip-flops?

Best movie ever? ______________

Worst movie ever? ______________

Favorite number? Why? ______________

- ○ Reality show ○ Sitcom?
- ○ Bicycle through Europe
- ○ African safari?

What scares you? ______________

Fave school subject? ______________

I LOVE TWISTER!

1. Name

2. Which have you taken a ride on? ○ Horse ○ Elephant ○ Camel ○ None!

3. Team(s) you like to root for? ____________________

4. Favorite pasta topping? ○ Meatballs ○ Cheese ○ Other____________

5. ○ Pencil ○ Pen ○ Keyboard?

6. Own a pair of boots? ○ No ○ Yes, ( ) pairs.

7. How 'bout a cowboy hat? ○ Yep ○ No way

8. Like peanut butter? ○ No ○ Yes, ____________ is my favorite kind.

9. Think quiet people are ○ smart ○ shy ○ not interested?

10. Ideal summer vacation? ____________________

11. Play a mean game of ping pong? ○ Yep, I'm awesome. ○ I'm OK. ○ No!

12. Last time you played Twister? ____________________

13. ○ Zoo ○ Aquarium ○ Neither, I like animals in the wild.

14. Do you like Scrabble? ○ Yes ○ No

15. Singer/Band that appears the most on your playlists? ____________

16. ZOMBIES ARE CHASING YOU. WHO DO YOU WANT WITH YOU? ____________

17. Huge sale at the mall. Who would you want with you? ____________

18. Tried raw oysters? ○ No ○ Yes Did you like? ○ No! Ick! ○ Yes

19. Three things for a perfect weekend? ____________________

20. Own anything with polka dots on it? ○ Of course ○ Nope

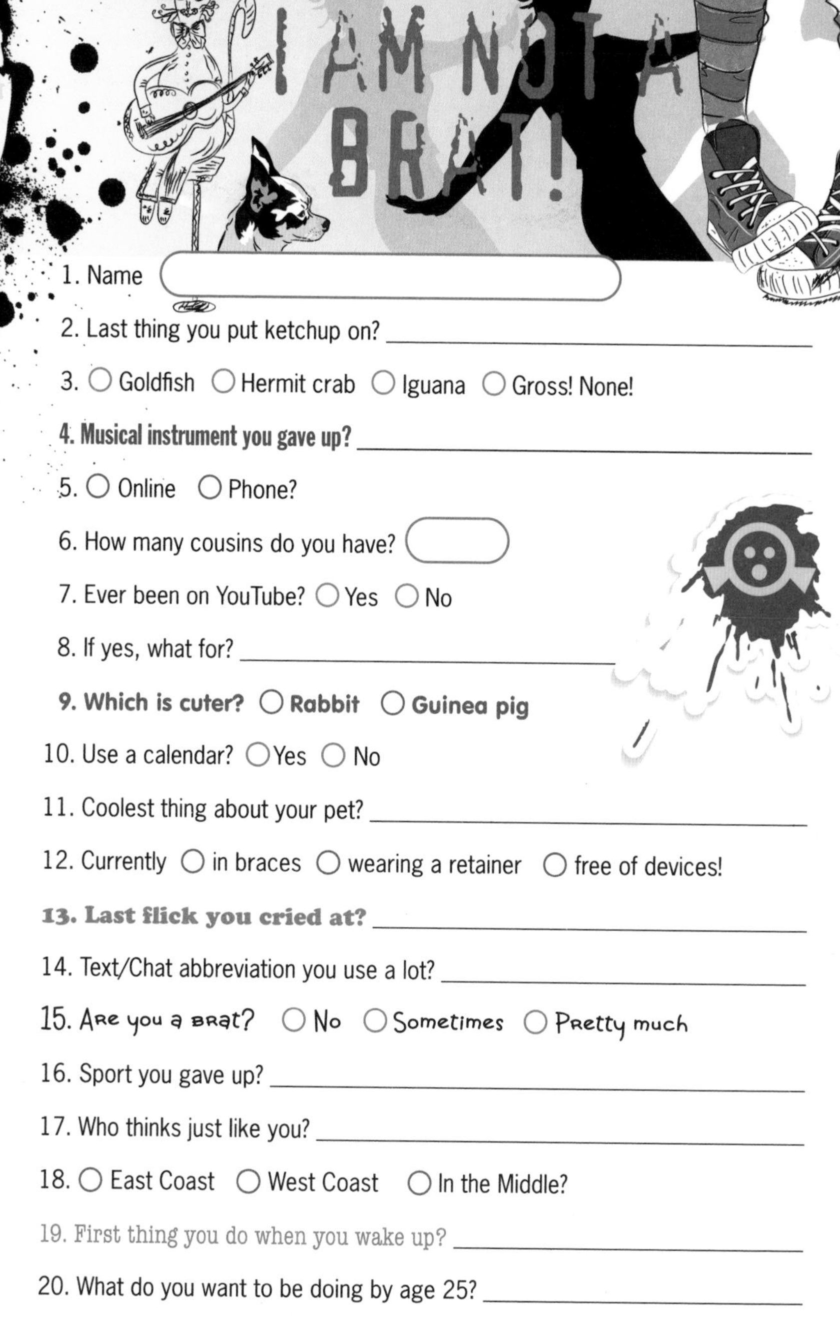

I AM NOT A BRAT!

1. Name

2. Last thing you put ketchup on? ______

3. ○ Goldfish ○ Hermit crab ○ Iguana ○ Gross! None!

4. **Musical instrument you gave up?** ______

5. ○ Online ○ Phone?

6. How many cousins do you have? ______

7. Ever been on YouTube? ○ Yes ○ No

8. If yes, what for? ______

9. **Which is cuter? ○ Rabbit ○ Guinea pig**

10. Use a calendar? ○ Yes ○ No

11. Coolest thing about your pet? ______

12. Currently ○ in braces ○ wearing a retainer ○ free of devices!

13. **Last flick you cried at?** ______

14. Text/Chat abbreviation you use a lot? ______

15. Are you a brat? ○ No ○ Sometimes ○ Pretty much

16. Sport you gave up? ______

17. Who thinks just like you? ______

18. ○ East Coast ○ West Coast ○ In the Middle?

19. First thing you do when you wake up? ______

20. What do you want to be doing by age 25? ______

named that?

Do you like it?

Yes

No

Fave thing that comes in a wrapper?

Would you rather ...

Swim like a dolphin

Fly like an eagle?

Can you tie a good bow?

Yes

No

Where would you swim to?

Where would you fly to?

Do you interrrupt people?

Yes ☹

No ☺

Shake

Malt

What IS malt?

Fave flave?

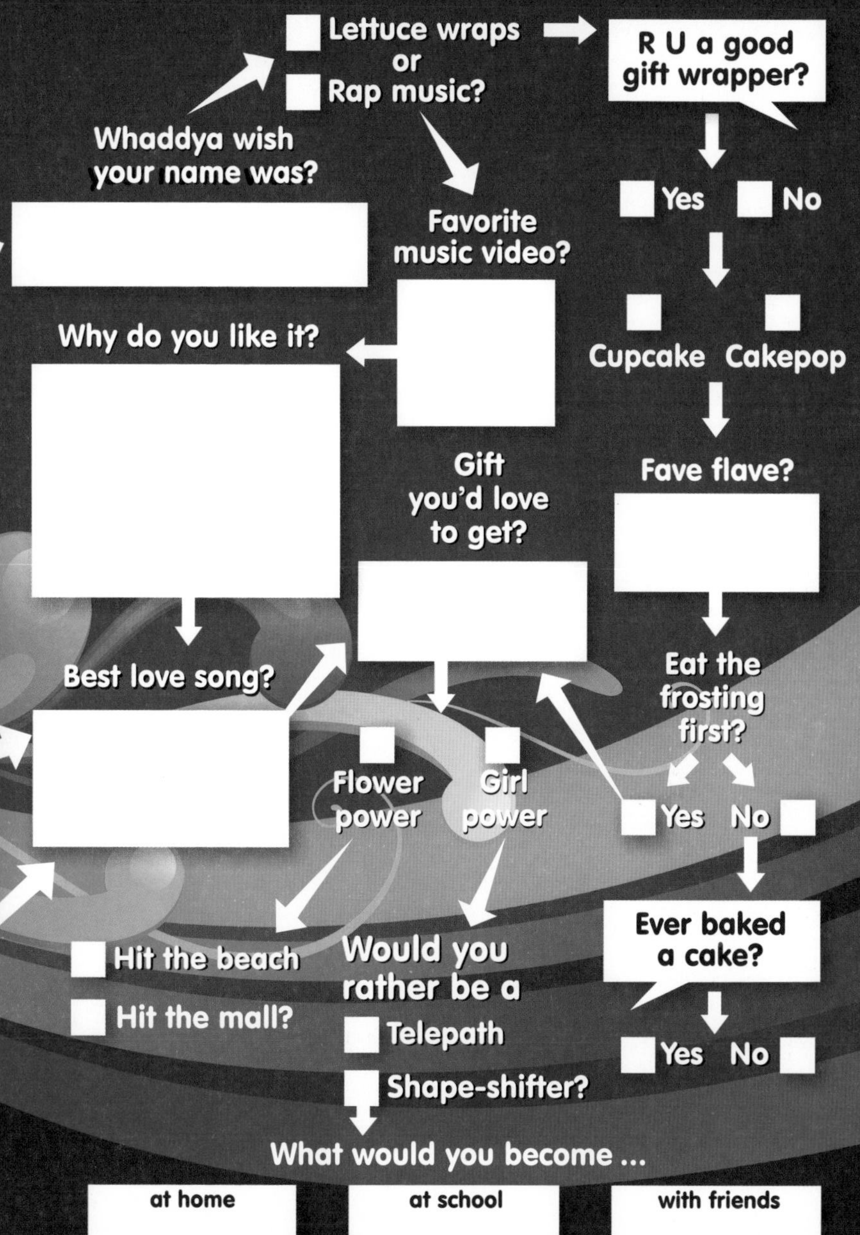

Lettuce wraps
or
Rap music?
R U a good gift wrapper?
Whaddya wish your name was?
Yes
No
Favorite music video?
Why do you like it?
Cupcake
Cakepop
Gift you'd love to get?
Fave flave?
Best love song?
Eat the frosting first?
Flower power
Girl power
Yes
No
Ever baked a cake?
Hit the beach
Hit the mall?
Would you rather be a
Telepath
Shape-shifter?
Yes
No
What would you become ...
at home
at school
with friends

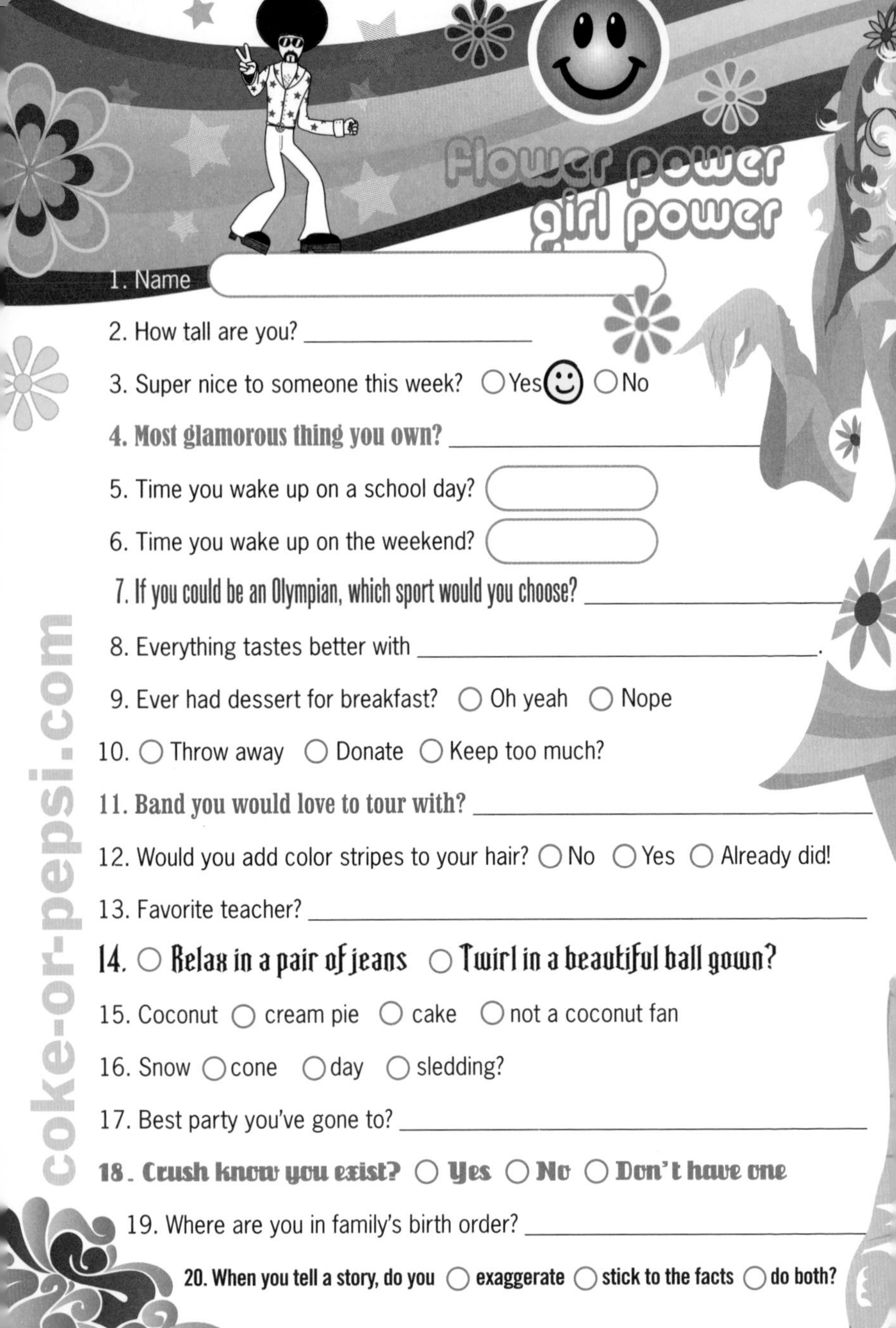

Flower power girl power

1. Name

2. How tall are you? ____________________

3. Super nice to someone this week? ○ Yes ○ No

4. **Most glamorous thing you own?** ____________________

5. Time you wake up on a school day?

6. Time you wake up on the weekend?

7. If you could be an Olympian, which sport would you choose? ____________________

8. Everything tastes better with ____________________.

9. Ever had dessert for breakfast? ○ Oh yeah ○ Nope

10. ○ Throw away ○ Donate ○ Keep too much?

11. **Band you would love to tour with?** ____________________

12. Would you add color stripes to your hair? ○ No ○ Yes ○ Already did!

13. Favorite teacher? ____________________

14. ○ Relax in a pair of jeans ○ Twirl in a beautiful ball gown?

15. Coconut ○ cream pie ○ cake ○ not a coconut fan

16. Snow ○ cone ○ day ○ sledding?

17. Best party you've gone to? ____________________

18. **Crush know you exist? ○ Yes ○ No ○ Don't have one**

19. Where are you in family's birth order? ____________________

20. **When you tell a story, do you ○ exaggerate ○ stick to the facts ○ do both?**

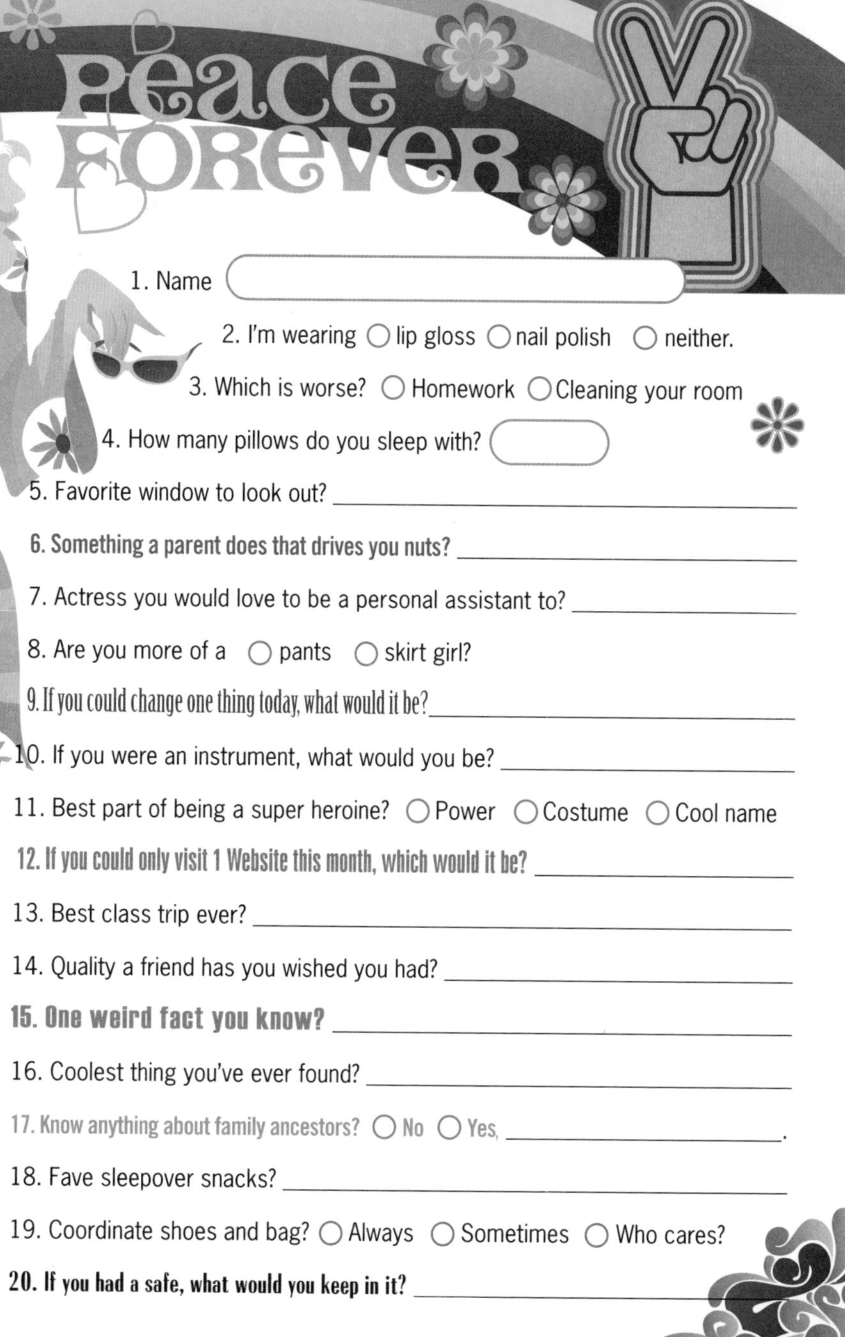

Peace Forever

1. Name

2. I'm wearing ◯ lip gloss ◯ nail polish ◯ neither.

3. Which is worse? ◯ Homework ◯ Cleaning your room

4. How many pillows do you sleep with?

5. Favorite window to look out? ______

6. Something a parent does that drives you nuts? ______

7. Actress you would love to be a personal assistant to? ______

8. Are you more of a ◯ pants ◯ skirt girl?

9. If you could change one thing today, what would it be? ______

10. If you were an instrument, what would you be? ______

11. Best part of being a super heroine? ◯ Power ◯ Costume ◯ Cool name

12. If you could only visit 1 Website this month, which would it be? ______

13. Best class trip ever? ______

14. Quality a friend has you wished you had? ______

15. One weird fact you know? ______

16. Coolest thing you've ever found? ______

17. Know anything about family ancestors? ◯ No ◯ Yes, ______.

18. Fave sleepover snacks? ______

19. Coordinate shoes and bag? ◯ Always ◯ Sometimes ◯ Who cares?

20. If you had a safe, what would you keep in it? ______

1. **a mermaid,** where in the world would you want to live? Why?

____

2. **President,** what kind of room would you add to the White House?

____

3. an exotic **animal keeper,** which animals would you want to care for?

____

4. **in charge** of naming the next kind of American spacecraft, what awesome name would you give it? _______________

5. **a dog,** which neighborhood dogs would you want to hang with? Why?

____

6. **a teacher,** what cool activity would you do with your class?

____

7. **in charge of your school** for a day, what would you change?

____

8. **going to live** on the moon for one year who would you take with you? Why? _______________

9. **able to stay** the same age for the rest of your life, which age would you pick? Why? _______________

10. able to have any **talent** you don't currently have, what would it be?

____

First thing that comes to mind when you see or hear these words?

(another word, sentence, or super short story)

1. Panda bear . . . .
2. Hysterical . . . .
3. Fireworks . . . .
4. T-shirt . . . .
5. Marshmallow . . . .
6. Celery sticks . . . .
7. Raisins . . . .
8. Poodle . . . .
9. Sunglasses . . . .
10. Chucks . . . .
11. Stick people . . . .
12. Physical Education . . . .
13. Mountain . . . .
14. Scooter . . . .
15. Pyramid . . . .
16. Diamonds . . . .
17. Hot peppers . . . .
18. Ringtone . . . .
19. Nail polish . . . .
20. Alligator . . . .

Name

1. Name

2. ○ Cinnamon ○ Fruity ○ Minty gum?

3. What do you love about yourself? ______________________

4. Where were you last time you used mustard? ______________________

5. The last paper I wrote for a class was about ______________________

____.

6. I could never eat ______________________ again and be OK.

7. TV show you most belong on? ______________________

8. WOULD YOU RATHER BE THE ○ STAR ON A LOSING TEAM ○ WORST ON A STAR TEAM?

9. Ever carved anything in a tree? ○ Yes ○ No

10. ○ Swim with the dolphins ○ Pet a manatee?

11. Would you rather be a ○ giant ○ pixie?

12. ○ **Fuzzy socks** ○ **Warm slippers?**

13. Hot chocolate ○ with ○ without marshmallows?

14. Good at sneaking up on people? ○ Not really ○ Kind of ○ Absolutely!

15. Scariest thing you've done on purpose? ______________________

16. New pair of ○ jeans ○ shoes?

17. **If I could ______________________, I would be thrilled.**

18. Age you turned on fave birthday?

19. Something you would love to see? ______________________

20. Which is worse? ○ Really sad ○ Out-of-control mad

Potato chips
French fries?
coke
OR
pepsi?
classic
Fashionable
Casual?
Sunset
Sunrise?
Brownies
Chocolate chip cookies?
Best holiday?
Fave actor?
Fave actress?
One word to describe you?
Big Mac
Whopper?
Gold
Silver?
coke-or-pepsi.com

orever

1. Name

2. ◯ Skinny jeans ◯ Jeggings ◯ Neither?

3. Happiest color? ______

4. What were you doing in the last photo taken of you? ______

5. Where were you? ______

6. Know how to cook? ◯ **No** ◯ **A little** ◯ **Yes**

7. If yes to #6, what's your specialty? ______

8. Are you usually ◯ cold ◯ hot?

9. Famous person you admire most? ______

10. DO HORROR MOVIES FRIGHTEN YOU? ◯ NOT REALLY ◯ YES, NIGHTMARES!

11. Fave outfit to relax in? ______

12. Ever shoot a spitball? ◯ Yes ◯ Gross, no!

13. Favorite thing that comes in your mail? ______.

14. Sprinkles ◯ always make me happy ◯ are kinda overrated.

15. Any phobias or fears? ◯ Nope ◯ Yes, I'm afraid of ______.

16. ◯ Drama queen ◯ Cool, calm, and collected?

17. What do you crave? ______

18. Drink after other people? ◯ Yeah ◯ Sometimes ◯ Never! Germs!

19. Ever encountered a bat? ◯ Yes ◯ No

20. What do you hear right now? ______

1. Name

2. Afraid to cross bridges? ◯ Yes ◯ No

3. Can you wiggle your ears without using your hands? ◯ No ◯ Yes

4. Do you ◯ give in ◯ get your way?

5. LAST THING YOU SOLD FOR YOUR SCHOOL? ____________

6. Go to the library? ◯ No ◯ Yes

7. Longest word you know? ____________

8. Can you hang a spoon from your nose? ◯ Yes ◯ No ◯ Huh?

9. Best food with a glass of milk? ____________

10. Gold ◯ fish ◯ bracelet?

11. Any strange talent? ◯ No ◯ Yes, I ____________.

12. Spend the night in a haunted house? ◯ NO! ◯ Sure, I don't believe.

13. It's scary how much I like ____________.

14. Give good manicures? ◯ Yes ◯ No

15. Favorite reality show? ____________

16. Scrambled eggs are ◯ yummy ◯ frightening.

17. Worst thing about your brother(s)/sister(s)? ____________

18. Best thing about your brother(s)/sister(s)? ____________

19. LOVE A GOOD MYSTERY? ◯ YES! ◯ NAH

20. Think you're creative? ◯ Yes ◯ A little ◯ Not really

Name

1. swim with a huge, harmless whale in the ocean, would you? ○Yes ○No, but I would swim with ____________________.

2. slow down time, which event would you slow down? ____________

3. add sisters or brothers to your family, which genders and ages would you choose? ____________________

4. have absolutely anything for dinner tonight, what would you pick? ____________

5. do one fun thing with an alien visiting our planet, what would it be? ____________

6. become any object for just one day, what would you be? Why? ____________

7. be an exchange student for one year anywhere in the world, which country would you visit? ____________

8. be great friends with someone from the past, who would you choose? Why? ____________

9. do absolutely anything for just one year, what would you do? ____________

10. change your last name, without hurting your parents' feelings, would you?
○ No ○ Yes, I would change it to ____________________.

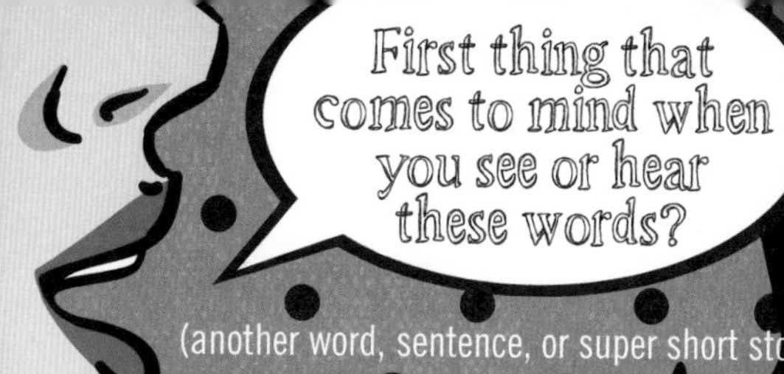

Name

1. Corn on the cob . . . .
2. Dark alley . . . .
3. Roller coaster . . . .
4. Pigs in blankets . . . .
5. Hamster . . . .
6. Pink . . . .
7. Glow-in-the-dark . . . .
8. The letter U . . . .
9. Hello Kitty . . . .
10. Face painting . . . .
11. Super star . . . .
12. Bell . . . .
13. Sleeping bag . . . .
14. Hollywood . . . .
15. Rock . . . .
16. Piano . . . .
17. Magazine . . . .
18. Watermelon . . . .
19. Bubbles . . . .
20. Subway . . . .

coke
OR
pepsi?
classic
Waffle cone
Sugar cone
Cup?
Ice cubes
Crushed ice?
TV
Book?
Beach
Mountains?
Go with the flow
Stick to a routine?
Ice cream
Fro-yo?
Favorite relative?
Best amusement park ride?
Favorite game?
Best book?
coke-or-pepsi.com

last things i painted were my nails

1. Name

2. Best thing in a spray can? ○ Whipped Cream ○ Cheese Whiz ○ Paint

3. Ever sprayed whipped cream directly in your mouth? ○ Yes ○ No

4. Last thing you painted? ____________________

5. Last thing you had stuck in your hair? ____________________

6. ○ Donuts ○ Donut holes

7. Worse T-shirt color? ○ Orange ○ Yellow ○ Green

8. What are you a beginner at? ____________________

9. What are you an expert at? ____________________

10. Favorite dip? ____________________

11. Favorite thing to dip? ____________________

12. Scarves? ○ Luv 'em ○ Hate 'em, so restricting!

13. I heart ____________________.

14. ____________________ is epic.

15. Friend with the coolest family? ____________________

16. ○ Red velvet cheesecake brownie ○ S'more-stuffed chocolate chip cookie?

17. Fave flave for lipgloss? ____________________

18. Favorite emoticon? ____________________

19. ○ Abracadabra ○ Bipiddi-boppidi-boo ○ Expelliarmus?

20. ○ Lemonade ○ Pink Lemonade?

PRIVATE

I like movies that make me cry

1. Name

2. Last animated movie you saw? ___

3. Movies ○ with happy endings ○ that leave you thinking?

4. Sleepovers? ○ Fun! ○ Ugh.

5. ○ French Bulldog ○ Irish Setter ○ Alaskan Husky?

6. **Movies ○ at the theater ○ at home?**

7. Are you a ○ share-your-umbrella ○ every-girl-for-herself kinda girl?

8. ○ Polo ○ Graphic Tee?

9. Love to see a ○ volcano erupt ○ total eclipse of the sun?

10. What does your hair do on rainy days? ___

11. **○ Write a great novel ○ Travel around the world?**

12. ○ Hike through the woods ○ Stroll through the city?

13. Ever danced the hula? ○ Yes ○ No

14. **Very first song you remember liking?** ___

15. Maple syrup on ○ waffles ○ French toast?

16. Ever fallen backwards in a chair? ○ Yes ○ No

17. **Wear shoes in the house? ○ Yes ○ Sometimes ○ Never**

18. If you get married, will you ○ keep ○ ditch ○ combine your last name(s)?

19. ○ Pack light ○ Certified overpacker?

20. FAVE SONG TO SING ON ROCK BAND OR GUITAR HERO? ___

I'll never get rid of my chucks

1. Name

2. On anyone's bad side right now? ◯ Yes ◯ No

3. WORN-OUT ITEM YOU CAN'T PART WITH? ______

4. ◯ Italian ice ◯ French vanilla ice cream ◯ German chocolate cake?

5. Most unusual animal you've ever fed? ______

6. When things get hard, do you usually ◯ give up ◯ keep trying?

7. SCHOOL UNIFORMS? ◯ FOR IT ◯ AGAINST?

8. ◯ Sweater ◯ Hoodie?

9. One thing you'd like to learn to do well? ______

10. Pigs are ◯ so cute ◯ muddy, stinky, and gross.

11. Wear glitter? ◯ Yes, love the sparkle! ◯ Nah, too gaudy.

12. Glow sticks? ◯ Still fun ◯ Ho hum

13. Last thing you do before you turn off the lights? ______

14. Love ◯ notes ◯ letter ◯ potion?

15. ◯ Brownie ◯ Girl Scout ◯ Other ______ ◯ None?

16. Favorite Girl Scout cookie? ______

17. Lucky charm or something lucky you wear? ◯ No ◯ Yes, ______.

18. Ever run a lemonade stand? ◯ Yes ◯ No

19. Kind of business you'd like to start someday? ______

20. **I would love to be president of** ______.

1. Name

2. Leopard prints are so ◯ chic ◯ tacky?

3. ◯ Seven dwarves ◯ One fairy godmother?

4. How many tiaras do you own?

5. Mannequins give you the creeps? ◯ No ◯ Yes

6. Ever been in a corn maze? ◯ Yes ◯ No ◯ Not sure, what is that?

7. Last school project you did? ____________________

8. British accents sound ◯ so cool ◯ smart ◯ kinda snobby?

9. ◯ Pair of glass slippers ◯ Pumpkin that turns into a carriage?

10. Magic ◯ potion ◯ wand ◯ markers?

11. ◯ Sand between your toes ◯ Out too deep to touch bottom?

12. Bowling? ◯ Ridiculous ◯ Fun ◯ Ridiculously fun!

13. What do you talk about more than anything? ____________________

14. Would you rather be a ◯ princess ◯ princess' sister?

15. Skinny jeans with ◯ flats ◯ flip-flops ◯ sneakers?

16. Today are you ◯ fairest of them all ◯ "sleepy" beauty?

17. Three words to describe your life? ____________________

18. Favorite song to sing with friends? ____________________

19. How 'bout to dance to with friends? ____________________

20. I wish I were a(n) ◯ English ◯ history ◯ math ◯ science whiz!

Who's the worst of the fairy tale foes?

- Wicked queen step-mother
- Super mean step-sisters
- Other

____

____

coke OR pepsi?

classic

- Coke
- Pepsi?

- Hot dog
- Hamburger?

- Milk
- Dark chocolate?

- Butterflies
- Dragonflies?

- Small talk
- Deep conversation?

- Sneakers
- Flip-flops?

Best movie ever? ______________

____

Worst movie ever? ______________

____

Favorite number? Why? ______________

____

- Reality show
- Sitcom?

- Bicycle through Europe
- African safari?

What scares you? ______________

____

Fave school subject? ______________

____

if you love
this book,
check out these
other
coke or pepsi?
books!

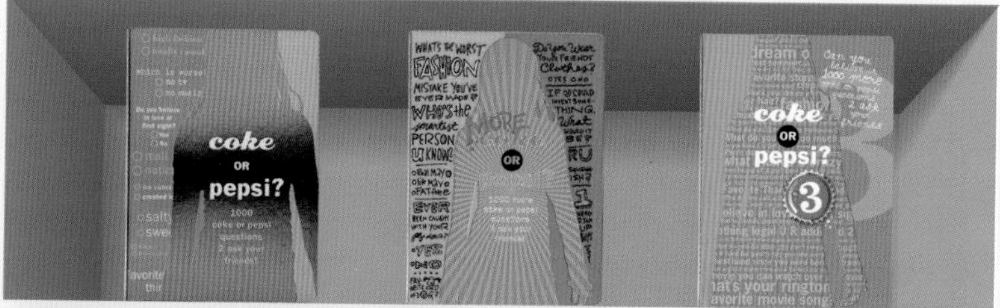

C or P